You
ARE AN
Awesome
Woman

Also by Becca Anderson

Let Me Count the Ways: Wise and Witty Women on the Subject of Love

Prayers for Calm: Meditations, Affirmations and Prayers to Soothe Your Soul

Badass Affirmations: The Wit and Wisdom of Wild Women

Badass Women Give the Best Advice: Everything You Need to Know About Life and Love

Think Happy to Stay Happy: The Awesome Power of Learned Optimism

Real Life Mindfulness: Meditations for a Calm and Quiet Mind

The Book of Awesome Women: Boundary Breakers, Freedom Fighters, Sheroes and Female Firsts

Prayers for Hard Times: Reflections, Meditations and Inspirations for Hope and Comfort

Everyday Thankful: Blessings, Graces and Gratitudes

You
ARE AN
Awesome
Woman

Affirmations and Inspired Ideas for
Self-Care, Success and a Truly Happy Life

Becca Anderson

author of the bestselling *Badass Affirmations*

CORAL GABLES

For permission requests, please contact the publisher at:

Mango Publishing Group

2850 S Douglas Road, 2nd Floor

Coral Gables, FL 33134 USA

info@mango.bz

For special orders, quantity sales, course adoptions and corporate sales, please email the publisher at sales@mango.bz. For trade and wholesale sales, please contact Ingram Publisher Services at customer.service@ingramcontent.com or +1.800.509.4887.

You Are An Awesome Woman: Affirmations and Inspired Ideas for Self-Care, Success and a Truly Happy Life

Originally published as Plan Be! by Mango Publishing Group, a Division of Mango Media, Inc.

Library of Congress Cataloging-in-Publication number: 2019944257

ISBN: (print) 978-1-64250-110-0, (ebook) 978-1-64250-111-7

BISAC category code SEL004000—SELF-HELP / Affirmations

Printed in the United States of America

This book is dedicated to all the amazing women from whom I have learned so much, and many of them are quoted here. Women helping other women will save the world!

"For love casts out fear, and gratitude
can conquer pride."

—Louisa May Alcott

Contents

$\mathcal{F}$OREWORD

By Alexandra Franzen

Founder/Editor, the Tiny Press Author,
You're Going to Survive and *The Checklist Book*

As a writer, I spend a great deal of time Googling all kinds of random, interesting topics—going down hundreds of spiraling internet rabbit-holes.

Occasionally, I stumble across a piece of information that leaves a permanent, forever-and-ever impression on my mind. After discovering this new piece of info, I perceive the world—and myself—differently.

Here's one of those.

Years ago, I came across a research study from a top university—a study about men, women, and confidence.

The premise was very simple.

First, the researchers divided their test subjects into two groups: male and female.

Everyone was given a fairly simple math test. Ten questions to complete.

After the test—before revealing the scores—the researchers asked the men, "So, how did it go? How well do you think you did on that test?" Generally, the men were quite confident about their scores. On average, the men replied, "Pretty good. I think I got about 8 or 9 out of 10 questions correct."

The women got asked the same question. On average, the women replied, "Oof, yikes, not so good. I think I got maybe 5 or 6 out of 10 questions correct."

Then the researchers revealed the actual scores. Turns out, everyone—male and female—performed *about the same*. The average test score was around 7 out of 10, regardless of gender.

Moral of the story: Often (not always, of course, there are exceptions to every rule…but often!) men tend to *slightly overestimate* their abilities ("I'm gonna do great!" "I've got this!" "I'm going for it!" "I'm a great candidate for this position!"), whereas women tend to *slightly underestimate* their abilities ("I don't think I'm qualified," "Why would they choose me?" "I'm not ready.")

What does this mean?

It means that, as a woman, you are actually *more awesome* than you think.

It's just that your tricky, annoying brain tries to convince you that you're not.

This pattern is prevalent in our world—not just with math tests, but in all realms of life.

Say, applying for a job. Studies on job-hunting show that women typically won't apply unless they meet close to 100 percent of the job criteria listed by the employer, whereas men will apply even if they meet far less than that.

Same with money. Surveys show that women are more reluctant to invest their money because they figure they won't be good at it, but then once they do, they tend to outperform male investors by .4 to 1.2 percent. (And when you're investing thousands, that slight percentage really adds up!)

Across the board, in so many areas of life, women tend to doubt their abilities more than men do, even when both are equally qualified. (And, even when women are *more* qualified!)

Google: "gender confidence gap" to read tons of fascinating articles on this topic.

To close this frustrating confidence gap, we need to re-train our brains. We need to release old beliefs and build new, better ones. This book can help with that.

Keep this book on your desk or bedside table. Open it often. Flip to a fresh page and read a few paragraphs or an inspirational quote. Let the words sink in. Let this book remind you, daily, that you are smarter, more capable, more creative, and more competent than you initially think.

Keep reminding yourself of this, daily. Remind your daughters, nieces, aunties, and girlfriends, too. Whenever you hear a woman doubting herself—"Can I really do this? Should I? Who cares what I have to say? I dunno, other people could probably do this better. I'm not strong enough. I don't have enough willpower. I don't think it's realistic…"—look her in the eyes and say, "Yes, you can. You are more prepared, more ready, and more qualified than you think. Go for it. Because you're awesome."

It's true. She is.
And you are, too.
Just like the title of this beautiful book affirms:

You are an awesome woman.

Even more awesome than you might realize. And
lightyears beyond.

Alexandra Franzen
October 29, 2019
Hilo, Hawaii

$\mathcal{I}$NTRODUCTION

You Are an Awesome Woman!
Secrets of Highly Successful Women

Women inspire me. It's as simple as that. All I have to do is look around. There are the women who run the restaurant on the corner—the place where everybody feels comfortable and taken care of. There are mothers pushing strollers, and mothers crunching numbers. There are women healing the sick. Gals cracking us up. Ladies penning the novels and singing the songs that change our lives. Chicks fixing the plumbing. Girls setting world records. Female politicians challenging the status quo from within the system, and activists battering it from the outside. There are women at the pinnacle of their fields in every corner of the world, and women finding satisfaction in their own successes, small and large. What's their secret? (Well, I'll give you a hint…there's more than one.)

What kind of success are you working toward? Maybe you don't know yet—or thought you did but aren't sure. Or maybe you're on the right track but need a kick in the pants.

In our own lives, success can feel elusive. We can get bogged down comparing ourselves to others or whining about what we lack. The women in this book have secrets to share, to shout to the rafters even. Their wise words will push your buttons, open your eyes, and rev up your engine.

This book is a reminder that you have what it takes to make it to the top. And the best part is, you get to decide where the top is, and you get to chart the path to reach it. This book is here for you—it's full of quotes and thoughts from hundreds of women to encourage, motivate, and support you as you make your way. Famous and infamous, wise and wisecracking, haughty and humble. Some are names you will know well, others are everyday gals like you and me with something important to add.

I read somewhere that we're all descended from three ancestral mothers. How amazing is that? A woman brought each and every one of us into this world, and when we look in the mirror, we can see traces of our mothers, grandmothers, even great-grandmothers. And their gifts go way beyond skin-deep. Every woman in the world is a member of this family—and you can call on their words and their life stories to inspire you at every turn. So keep this book close to you as you get organized, vamp up your personal style, and figure out how to work smarter. Sit back and let this book help you remember the importance of relaxing and indulging yourself (with girlfriends whenever possible). And don't ever forget to go after your dreams with every ounce of yourself because after all—women can do anything!

The Art of Self-Affirmation

If you find yourself feeling overwhelmed and drained by the busyness of life and its many demands, you need to stop in your tracks and do an attitude adjustment, or more specifically, a "gratitude adjustment." Whenever you have gotten to this point, you have need of some "me TLC" and a dose of radical self-care. Chances are, your very wonderfulness may have led you to give and give and give and give. Now, you need to give and give and give to yourself. You need to soak up the glory of your very being and remember that you are an amazing, awesome person who is deserving of all good things!

The world is changing all around us with increasing speed, making most of us feel we have no control. We are so busy doing and being productive and bullet journaling our way through life that we might be riding in the passenger seat of our own car. I am a positive living and affirmation queen, but I've definitely been to the edge of overwhelm and back again. While on my journey, I've gathered a lot of wisdom, and here is my big takeaway:

If you affirm yourself every day, you can rule the world. More importantly, you can live a life filled with love, joy, fulfillment, and satisfaction thanks to your own positive self-regard.

Through the art of daily self-affirmation, you can take control of your own destiny and create your ideal life. If it sounds easy, it can be, but it does require you to develop the discipline to reflect on a positive affirmation each day. These affirmations are a mindfulness practice that will strengthen your self-esteem. Like a muscle, the more you do it, the stronger your confidence and sense of self will be. *You Are An Awesome Woman* is the ultimate motivating, encouraging, and uplifting book to enjoy and share. These very wise words and affirmative sayings have the power to touch our hearts, make us laugh, and alleviate our stress as we realize the vast potential life has to offer. Grouped together, these quips, quotes, and "power thoughts" can help you deal with everything life throws at you with élan. Simply put, you'll be too blessed to be stressed!

How to Use This Book

Pick up the book, randomly open to a quote, and let those words be your guiding thought for the day. If this power thought *really* resonates with you, keep using it every day and let it become your mantra.

Use these inspired ideas in speeches, on your bulletin board, in your email signature, and on your Twitter handle and social media platforms. Hey, if it is your favorite Big Thought ever, get a tattoo on your inner wrist where you'll see it all the time and be reminded of your personal worth and of the great big beautiful world we all live in.

Read a few and really "power up" for your day, sort of like a booster shot in word form. If you are getting ready for a presentation, a sales pitch, an interview for your dream job, your next YouTube taping, or any very important date, these affirmations and words of wisdom can be the wind in your sails.

Just love the heck out of yourself *every* day!

CHAPTER ONE

Organization Is the Key to Happiness

Do you come home every night and feel a bit guilty about the stacks and piles of clutter? Is something blocking your creativity or the get-up-and-go you need for all your household projects? Does your energy feel "stuck" in certain rooms, even impeding a good night's sleep in your own bed? Is your desk or workstation hopelessly cluttered? Do you go out or order in dinner all the time, not even wanting to cook in your own kitchen? If any of this rings true, I wrote this book for you.

Your home and office should feel like a sanctuary. We should be able to walk in the front door and immediately feel a sense of comfort, refuge, and safe haven. There are lots of things you can do, both large and small, that will make a tangible difference in the way your home feels and functions. Getting rid of anything you no longer use will increase the functionality of your home by making it easier to clean, increase orderliness, and improve energy. I made a breakthrough discovery two years ago when I decided to unpack boxes I had never opened since moving in six years before. While they were tucked away, unseen in the basement storage area, I knew they were there. One weekend, I decided to take the plunge and open those boxes. Going through our things can be an emotional experience; I remember finding a card from a friend who had passed away and immediately becoming misty-eyed. Powered by a triple latte, I plowed through the boxes and placed objects into three designated areas: Donate, Trash, and Keep. The goal was to have as little in the "Keep" zone as possible. I am proud to say that even less was in the trash, and that was only a few items that had broken during the move. "Donate" became several carloads to the Recycle and Reuse Center. Once I got the knack of it, most of the "Keep" pile ended up there, too. After the whirl of activity, something unexpected happened: I felt suddenly very buoyant and much lighter. I realized those unopened boxes had caused an invisible cloud of guilt; they had weighed me down. When the cloud lifted, I experienced a kind of effervescent joy. It was simply wonderful. I ask you, what might be holding you back from being utterly happy at home or at work?

If managing your life feels like a war, then half of every battle is getting things in order. For me, it's no fun at all. I have this nagging feeling that I have two lives going on simultaneously: the fun stuff and the rest of it. For example, I love to cook but despise washing dishes. I love the feeling of paying off the monthly bills, but often can't get myself together to do it until a week past the deadline, and then I feel miserable about the cumulative effect on my credit score. And any upheaval—a move, an emergency, or just getting a bad head cold—throws me for a loop. *How did I let this go?!* I ask myself, crazed. *Why is my house filled with paper?!* (One in every five pieces is really important, I swear.)

Well, it's time for a detox, a deep cleansing, and a spring cleaning. Doing your taxes. Clearing and sorting your wardrobe. Getting rid of the magazines you've been unwittingly storing since college. What a wonderful release. Now, those are the big projects, and don't worry yourself into trying to do them all at once. Just pick a project each month and do it a little at a time, or else set aside a whole weekend to blast through, whatever suits your style.

And for the rest of the month, take aim at the little, repetitive, everyday stuff. Work hard to make it a habit to sort your mail right away, clean out your pockets and purse every day, and dream up new ways to multitask effectively. Train yourself to make a difference in tiny ways all day long, and soon you'll forget it's an annoyance because when it all adds up, you're way ahead of the game. If you can coax yourself into making the art of organization second nature, I promise it will serve you forever.

Find Your Focus

You may not be able to foresee what the universe
has planned for you, but that doesn't mean your
own plans should be unpredictable.

SANDRA OLIVER

Sometimes I still lose my head, even though it is
attached to my body. But if I've left myself a note,
I can usually find it again.

MARLO THOMAS

Detail is electric.

BONNI GOLDBERG

To know where you can find a thing is the
chief part of learning.

UNKNOWN

Only when your consciousness is totally focused on
the moment you are in can you receive whatever
gift, lesson, or delight that moment has to offer.

BARBARA DE ANGELIS

On clutter: chaos begets chaos in our homes,
and in our minds.

CAROL WISEMAN

A place for everything, and everything in its place.

ISABELLA MARY BEETON

Just before bedtime prayers, evaluate each day.
Make plans for tomorrow that will move you toward
your long-range goal.

FLORENCE S. JACOBSEN

✦

Words are a lens to focus one's mind.

AYN RAND

✦

Most of what you obtain in life will be because
of your discipline. Discipline is perhaps more
important than ability.

CHRISTINE DARDEN

Never walk into or out of a meeting without
a clear agenda.

MARY JANE RYAN

✦

Many a woman has a "to-do" list that resembles the
phone book! Don't overdo your "to-do" list. Keep it
reasonable and keep it doable.

LESLIE ROSSMAN

✦

Write out your problem on a piece of paper, stick
the paper in a drawer, and close it. Do not allow
yourself to look at or think about the list until the
end of the week. By then, you may look at your
problems differently and will have solutions.

MICHELLE STRONG

✦

I don't wait for moods. You accomplish nothing
if you do that. Your mind must know it has got to
get down to work.

PEARL S. BUCK

PLAN AND PREPARE

Look twice before you leap.

CHARLOTTE BRONTË

The very best impromptu speeches are the ones
written well in advance.

RUTH GORDON

What I've learned from fairy tales: Invest in some
good string rather than breadcrumbs. That
way, you can always find the path back to the
gingerbread house.

WENDY ST. CHARLES

Failing to plan is planning to fail.

EFFIE JONES

If one asks for success and prepares for failure, she
will get the situation she has prepared for.

FLORENCE SCOVEL SHINN

Don't agonize. Organize.

FLORYNCE KENNEDY

✦

Plans are necessary to life and achievement in
any sphere. But they should never overcome our
powers of flexibility.

DIXIE MARTIN

✦

Lack of confidence is born from a lack of preparation.

SHANNON WILBURN

✦

Luck is a matter of preparation meeting opportunity.

OPRAH WINFREY

✦

You had better live your best and act your best
and think your best today; for today is the sure
preparation for tomorrow and all the other
tomorrows that follow.

HARRIET MARTINEAU

Winning is the science of being totally prepared.

GRACIE ALLEN

✦

Preparation, I have often said, is rightly two-thirds
of any venture.

AMELIA EARHART

Dream On!

Fantasies are more than substitutes for unpleasant
reality; they are also dress rehearsals, plans. All acts
performed in the world begin in the imagination.

BARBARA GRIZZUTI HARRISON

What the world really needs is more love
and less paperwork.

PEARL BAILEY

✦

If we would only give, just once, the same amount
of reflection to what we want to get out of life
that we give to the question of what to do with a
two weeks' vacation, we would be startled at the
aimless procession of our busy days.

DOROTHY CANFIELD FISHER

I want to so order my life that its impression,
its impact, might always be positive and
spiritually constructive.

DOROTHY BROWN

For the happiest life, days should be rigorously
planned, nights left open to chance.

MIGNON MCLAUGHLIN

To stay ahead, you must have your next idea
waiting in the wings.

ROSABETH MOSS KANTER

All the flowers of all the tomorrows are in the
seeds of today.

PROVERB

Make big plans; aim high in hope and work,
remembering that a noble and logical
plan never dies, but long after we are gone
will be a living thing.

LITA BANE

It's never too late—in fiction or in life—to revise.

NANCY THAYER

Take Your Life in Your Own Hands

It's true that life's gifts come with responsibilities. When I don't feel like cleaning up my desk or my car or my house or my general existence, I try to remember the people who would be desperate to have all the things I take for granted.

RACHEL CLARKSON

✦

You take your life in your own hands, and what happens? A terrible thing: no one to blame.

ERICA JONG

✦

Make decisions in a timely fashion—rarely does waiting improve the quality of the decision.

ODETTE POLLAR

This is a wonderful world for women. The richness,
the hope, the promise of life today…are exciting
beyond belief. Nonetheless, we need stout hearts
and strong characters; we need knowledge and
training; we need organized effort to meet the future.

BELLE S. SPAFFORD

✦

When planning for a year, plant corn.When
planning for a decade, plant trees. When planning
for life, train and educate people.

CHINESE PROVERB

✦

I don't know that there are any shortcuts
to doing a good job.

SANDRA DAY O'CONNOR

✦

I was taught the way of progress is neither
swift nor easy.

MARIE CURIE

Some Helpful How-Tos

I must govern the clock, not be governed by it.

GOLDA MEIR

If only everything were as easily organized as, say,
my shoe collection. And even that can sometimes
be a losing battle.

SASHA MORROW

There are so many options, so much to do, so many
demands on women. There is no point in taking
one hour to do a ten-minute task, nor should we
slap together an hour-worthy project in ten minutes.

ELAINE CANNON

Arrange whatever pieces come your way.

VIRGINIA WOOLF

✦

A team is more than a collection of people. It is a
process of give and take.

BARBARA GLACEL

Effective teamwork is all about making a good, well-balanced salad, not whipping individuals into a single batch of V8.

SANDRA RICHARDSON

✦

Take just a few minutes each day to sort through any miscellaneous papers on your desk at home or the office, rather than letting unorganized piles multiply and grow.

GLADYS MORISSON

✦

To achieve your dreams, remember your ABC's: **A**void negative sources, people, places, things, and habits. **B**elieve in yourself. **C**onsider things from every angle.

WANDA HOPE CARTER

✦

Keep things as simple as possible…nobody wants to reorganize their system of reorganization!

CASSIE LAWRENCE

✦

If a problem has no solution, it's not a problem, just a fact.

BJ GALLAGHER

There are two ways of meeting difficulties. You alter the difficulties or you alter yourself to meet them.

PHYLLIS BOTTOMED

✦

Adopt the highly effective SAW inbox system: ["S" for] STAT (as in a hospital emergency room) means "do it now!" and is for urgent tasks with a deadline of today. "A" stands for "as soon as possible" and goes on your to-do list with doable deadlines. "W" stands for "whenever" and is only for ideas and wishes for the future.

ROBERTA LEFFLER

✦

I always say don't make plans, make options.

JENNIFER ANISTON

One way to keep control over the paper in your life is to get it back in circulation. Do you have a stack of magazines that you are almost done with? Take a few moments to go through them, and then pass them on to friends, a library, a school, a hospital, or a charity thrift shop. I have a magazine "trade" system set up with some girlfriends!

LILLIAN CRIST

Get a 3-ring binder with pocketed dividers for receipts and user manuals, and organize by need such as "birthdays," "utility bills," "credit cards and reports," "computer info," and most importantly, "taxes!"

NINA LESOWITZ

The most successful people in the world break big tasks down into doable pieces. If you have a major goal that feels overwhelming to you—slice and dice it. One step at a time and the mountain is climbed—now, doesn't that feel great?

DEENA PATEL-WINE

I make the most of all that comes and the least of all that goes.

SARA TEASDALE

Never rely just on your smartphone or a file on your computer to safely store your mailing addresses, numbers, and email addresses. Just one computer crash or loss of your smartphone can render you helpless if you lack backups, whether to the cloud, a hard copy, or thumb drives in safe remote locations!

SUZANNA HARWELL

Less Can Truly Be More

You should only have possessions you really love; don't let your things possess you. I have a neat-looking "outbox" on my front porch that I fill during the week with items I can take to the Reuse Center at my neighborhood recycling location. As the days go by, magazines, extra pots and pans, odd cups and dishes, old electronics, and any things that no longer have a place in my home go there. My partner and I go there at least twice a month, and it simply feels wonderful. The center has a lot of regulars, and we are now recognized as purveyors of 100 percent discount bounty, such as scented candles, barely-worn scarves, office supplies, crockery, and superb magazines, as we are a household of voracious readers. I have seen amazing trades at the Reuse Center, and I witnessed a musician sitting down and playing a free sitar with virtuosity while a family with young children got a sorely needed washing machine and dryer. Moments like this remind me of a novel by the visionary teacher and writer Starhawk; *The Fifth Sacred Thing* depicts a future where people return to a barter system and live harmoniously in community.

Take only what you need and share anything extra with your own neighbors.

Chapter Two

Self-Care: Love Yourself
So You Can Love Your Life

Be kind to yourself, too. Make a commitment to yourself
to refrain from negative self-talk. Be kind to yourself and
focus on the traits you like rather than the ones you don't.
The extremely wise Dawna Markova, the author of some of
my favorite books, including *I Will Not Die an Unlived Life*,
says, "Your soul remembers when you put yourself down; it
imprints upon you. Never do this. Self-compassion is key to
a life well-lived." How can you take better care of yourself?

You know the feeling too well: you're worn out. The end
of the rope you're dangling from is frayed and about to
snap. But you can't stop. Your to-do list is longer than the
beginnings of that novel you've been working on, and every
second that ticks by is gone forever. STOP! You're no good
to anyone in this state—not to your boss, your best friends,
your family, and most of all, yourself.

In high school, I was a bit of an overachiever, wearing myself
to the bone to get good grades and participate in every
extracurricular activity I could. Overall, I enjoyed it, but I
remember waking up one morning and having my mother

tell me I should stay home from school. I wasn't really sick, but I was exhausted. I didn't know what to make of it—most parents would punish their kids for trying to get out of going to school. But her lesson was partly about perspective. If I was sacrificing my health and my sanity for things that were meant to be fulfilling and fun, what was the point? And she knew better than I that some downtime would refresh me, and then I could hit the ground running the next day doing what I loved.

Naps. Walks. Quiet time. Meditation. Breathing. Daydreaming. Baths. A good book. Or maybe best of all, doing nothing. When's the last time you took a step back and really took a moment for yourself? It's about time. Here are a few famous quotes as well as some tried-and-true suggestions from ladies like you and me for taking good care of number one.

Slow Down

If you realize too acutely how valuable time is, you
are too paralyzed to do anything.

KATHARINE BUTLER HATHAWAY

✦

To achieve the impossible dream, try going to sleep.

JOAN KLEMPNER

✦

Like kids, adults need time-outs too, but it's usually
to keep from doing something bad rather than
as punishment.

KATHY FREEMAN

✦

A good rest is half the work.

PROVERB

✦

Relaxation is an art that has been made very difficult
to practice by the conditions of modern civilization.

ALANIS MORISSETTE

For fast-acting relief, try slowing down.

LILY TOMLIN

Regardless of your religion, go inside a local church, temple, or synagogue and sit for a half an hour when there is no service happening. Simply sit and enjoy the company of your thoughts, the mellow lighting, and the reflective atmosphere.

JAY KHAN

If you don't take naps, take one! Take a nap in the middle of the day when you are unusually overwhelmed. Just doing this once during an "off limits" time will renew your sense of self and allow you to stay on task the rest of the time!

DONNA OLICKIN

✦

Take a bath early in the morning, before you begin your daily routine. Get up earlier if you have to and immerse yourself in the tub. You will have a relaxed day.

POLLY PORTER

Interrupt your daily routine on a weekend by doing *nothing*; it brings a fresh perspective.

CAROL WISEMAN

Laugh Out Loud

You grow up the day you have your first real laugh at yourself.

ETHEL BARRYMORE

Housework can't kill you, but why take a chance?

PHYLLIS DILLER

Remember that thing they say about stopping and counting to ten? It only works if you're sane enough to count.

ALEX PRESTON

✦

I am woman! I am invincible! I am pooped!

BJ GALLAGHER

Insanity is my only means of relaxation.

VARLA VENTURA

Read some young adult fiction—a Nancy Drew book or anything by Lemony Snicket. Get yourself out of the busy adult world and remember what it was like to get lost in a book.

EVELYN VANDERMERE

Here is the opposite of your "to-do" list for work! Make an "I want to do this" list. It can be as adventurous as possible, anything you want to accomplish in your life: plant a gorgeous garden, go to Australia and surf, learn to play piano, hang glide. Just by making the list, you are helping your wild wishes come true!

LOTTE WARNER

Learn and Share

Love the moment, and the energy of that moment
will spread beyond all boundaries.

SISTER CORITA KENT

Take up a new hobby you've always been
interested in. Learning a new skill will make
you feel productive, even if that skill is only for
your enjoyment.

LAURA BAKER

Don't forget the simple pleasures of your past.
Recently I remembered a favorite present from my
childhood, an origami kit. I bought myself a new kit
and was delighted to find that making these tiny
works of art can still focus and clear my mind.

MABLE EVANS

A change of scenery is often the easiest way to take time away from our everyday lives. Never underestimate the benefits of a simple day trip alone or with friends.

REBECCA GLEESOB

A potluck with friends may be a simple tradition, but it's one of the most fun and even rewarding to uphold.

FLORENCE ALLEN

Museums are some of the best places to gain a bit of relaxation and perspective. You have to think about something besides your own problems when surrounded by the evidence of so much other reality.

CANDICE LONG

Listen to music you like, and cultivate that interest actively—go to concerts, listen to CDs you have never heard at the store, and share your taste with friends. Music communicates to us on many different levels, and your favorite music tends to transport your mind to its favorite place.

KIMBERLY LYNN DAVIS

Develop your green thumb—even if you only have a couple of pots on your deck or fire escape. Learn all about plants online or at the local nursery, and add seasonal plants for spring and fall. Not only will you be creating beauty, you will be more in tune with nature and the seasons.

RUTH BAXTER

Pets are great happiness boosters. The companionship, love, and entertainment a pet provides is for many people as significant as any human relationship. Medical researchers have even discovered that petting your pets reduces blood pressure!

SHELLY STRONG

Grab your wild friends and have a clothing swap. Set aside clothes or accessories you don't wear, gather with friends who've done the same, and begin a fair trade. Spice up your wardrobe without spending money!

DEE LOGAN

Let It Go

Forget the past and live the present hour.

SARAH KNOWLES BOLTON

The jump is so frightening between where I am and where I want to be…because of all I may become, I will close my eyes and leap!

MARY ANNE RADMACHER

Worry does not empty tomorrow of its sorrow; it empties today of its strength.

CORRIE TEN BOOM

You can always find reasons to work. There will always be one more thing to do. But when people don't take time out, they stop being productive. They stop being happy, and that affects the morale of everyone around them.

CARISA BIANCHI

Wrinkles are called worry lines for a reason.

JANICE THOMPSON

Stress is an ignorant state. It believes that
everything is an emergency. Nothing is
that important.

NATALIE GOLDBERG

Tension is who you think you should be. Relaxation
is who you are.

CHINESE PROVERB

If only we'd stop trying to be happy we'd have a
pretty good time.

EDITH WHARTON

Lose track of time—on a weekend, declare it a "no
watch" weekend! Notice how much more relaxed
you will be if you are not always looking at your
watch. Ahhhh.

JULIE HENNESSY

$\mathcal{S}$IMPLIFY

Life isn't a matter of milestones but of moments.

ROSE FITZGERALD KENNEDY

There is no need to go to India or anywhere else to find peace. You will find that deep place of silence right in your room, your garden, or even your bathtub.

ELISABETH KÜBLER-ROSS

To sit in the shade on a fine day and look upon verdure is the most perfect refreshment.

JANE AUSTEN

The sound of birds stops the noise in my mind.

CARLY SIMON

Sometimes the most important thing in a whole day is the rest we take between two long breaths, or the turning inwards in prayer for five short minutes.

ETTY HILLESUM

Like water which can clearly mirror the sky and the trees only so long as its surface is undisturbed, the mind can only reflect the true image of the Self when it is tranquil and wholly relaxed.

INDRA DEVI

If you can attain repose and calm, believe that you have seized happiness.

JULIE-JEANNE-ELEONORE DE LESPINASSE

Turn off the television and the radio in your car, office, and home for one full day. Allow yourself to listen to the silence.

VICTORIA MARTUCCI

To instantaneously relax, slowly take four deep inhales and exhales. Just focus on your breath and slowly count to three as you breathe.

JEAN MCINTYRE

Working in the garden gives me something beyond the enjoyment of senses. It gives me a profound sense of inner peace.

RUTH STOUT

One way to really relax is with a warm mug of herbal tea—chamomile is one of the most relaxing of all, while peppermint both stimulates and calms. An orange and rose hip tea is good for unwinding and also adds a healthy dose of vitamin C, too!

ANALEYAH NORTH

CREATE CALM

Taking time for yourself should never be seen as a burden. Not on you, and not on anyone else.

ELIZABETH FRANKLIN

People tell you to take care of yourself like it's an easy thing. It's not. It's a very hard thing sometimes, but there's no shame in making the effort.

FAITH WALKER

Daily walks are one of my best discoveries. It's just about the only thing I can do for forty-five minutes without being interrupted.

FREIDA RAMONE

Take some time for yourself every single day.
Even if it's just five minutes. Even if you have to
lock the door.

CASSIDY SNOW

✦

It may be a cliché, but there often is nothing better
than preparing something special to eat. Not for
your family or your friends, just for you.

FRANCINE LOVETT

✦

Designate one day a month as Retreat Day. Turn off
your phones, radio, television, and computer. Read.
Cook yummy food. Sit in silence. Enjoy!

DREW BARRYMORE

✦

Take a walk on your lunch hour!

DEBRA POBLETE

After washing your hair, allow it to dry
naturally in the sun.

MADELEINE SOMERVILLE

Give yourself flowers—and really do it! The longest lasting blooms are sunflowers, Peruvian lilies, and dahlias. Most importantly, getting the flowers will bring the biggest smile to your face.

ELISE MARIE COLLINS

Buy yourself a new loofah, a back brush, or a new washcloth and body wash with lavender essential oil. Use it!

FRAN PETERSON

Take yourself out to dinner.

STACY LEVINE

Get a life! People who excel have a life outside of work, which makes them happier, and therefore, more efficient!

PAYTON ROBINSON

Only when one is connected to one's own core is one connected to others. And for me, the core, the inner spring, can be best refound through solitude.

ANNE MORROW LINDBERGH

If you're usually surrounded by people, spend a
day all by yourself and enjoy the solitude—and the
deliciousness—of your own company.

CYNTHIA MACGREGOR

Rewire Your Brain to Be More Positive

Neuropsychiatrist David Amen, MD, posits that thoughts
carry physical properties and that the properties of
negative thoughts can be detrimental to your leading a
healthy, happy life. To overturn these negative effects,
he prescribes thinking more positively, maintaining that
by doing so, you can change the way your brain works
and in turn, change your life for the better.

ℭhapter 𝒯hree

Express Yourself Through Your Personal Style

The essence of your style is all you. It sounds obvious, even silly. But how often do we flip through a magazine or look at others on the street and long to have some other woman's wardrobe, body, or charisma? The best make it look effortless, but we know it rarely is. The great thing about true style is that it stands on its own, and you don't have to judge or envy anyone else to get it *because it's already yours*. Every outfit you admire, every color that lights up your face, every pair of shoes you flip for—they all reflect you at your best, ready to take on the world.

My best friend claims that whenever she's going through a major transformation—being fired or quitting a job, ending a relationship, or starting a move—she buys one thing that seems outlandish for the circumstances. Something she may feel she can't quite afford, but that she absolutely loves and will treasure for a long time. She calls it her I'll-never-[work/be happy/fall in love]-again dress, and considers it a kind of reverse psychology good luck charm. The thinking goes that if she's all washed up, at least she has this one last beautiful thing to remember as she wallows in her misery. Of course, she's not one to wallow. And I think the true purpose is to force herself back into the game by embracing beauty in her own way and on her own terms. It cheers her right up to tote around a new bag or get compliments on an inspired new 'do. And let me tell you, it works for her…she's never been down in the dumps for long (and even if she was, she sure wouldn't look it).

After conducting an informal poll of the most stylish women I know, I've put together the 1-2-3 rules. (And of course, the best of the best know how to outdo themselves by breaking every rule.)

1. Simplicity is the key—especially on a budget. Clean lines, strong colors, no fuss.

2. Always feel comfortable in your clothes—if you love the way it looks on the hanger but feel funny every time you put it on, it goes right into the clothes swap pile.

3. Quality over quantity—for the price of a lot of cheap stuff that wears out in one season, buy one great thing you'll have forever.

Express Your Inner Beauty

I think your whole life shows in your face and you
should be proud of that.

LAUREN BACALL

Style may be on the surface, but you can be deep
and still have some.

CLARISSA GOUGH

Looking for a new sense of style? Try a new sense of
self first. It's cheaper, and you won't have to get rid
of the impulse buys.

RHONDA BRADFORD

✦

Kindness is always fashionable.

AMELIA BARR

✦

Fashion is not something that exists in dresses only.
Fashion is in the sky, in the street, fashion has to do
with ideas, the way we live, what is happening.

COCO CHANEL

Fashion can be bought. Style one must possess.

EDNA WOOLMAN CHASE

✦

Beauty is how you feel inside, and it reflects in your eyes. It is not something physical.

SOPHIA LOREN

✦

Fashions are always changing, but our friendships will never go out of style.

REEDA JOSEPH

✦

Style is based on who you are.

ISABELLA ROSSELLINI

✦

What about saying, "This is how I look, and I'm beautiful and I'm strong." You're not going to be what everybody loves. But you have to love yourself. Making the decision to do that is something you can actually do.

AMY SCHUMER

Of all the things you wear, your expression is the most important.

JANET LANE

How many cares one loses when one decides not to be something but to be someone.

COCO CHANEL

There is no cosmetic for beauty like happiness.

MARIA MITCHELL

Show Your Sass

If the shoe fits, it's too expensive.

ADRIENNE GUSOFF

✦

If high heels were so wonderful, men would be wearing them.

SUE GRAFTON

I base my fashion taste on what doesn't itch.

GILDA RADNER

✦

We are entitled to wear cowboy boots to our
own revolution.

NAOMI WOLF

✦

Some women hold up dresses that are so ugly, and
they always say the same thing: 'This looks much
better on.' On what? On fire?

RITA RUDNER

✦

The only rule is don't be boring… Life is too short
to blend in.

PARIS HILTON

✦

Give a girl the correct footwear and she can
conquer the world.

BETTE MIDLER

I'm not offended by all the dumb blonde jokes because I know I'm not dumb. I also know I'm not blonde.

DOLLY PARTON

✦

Dear, NEVER forget one little point: It's MY business. You just work here.

ELIZABETH ARDEN
(IN A NOTE TO HER HUSBAND)

✦

I'm a big woman. I need big hair.

ARETHA FRANKLIN

✦

I wouldn't say I invented tacky, but I definitely brought it to its present high popularity.

BETTE MIDLER

Shop Til You Drop. Pamper Til You're Pooped

I would rather shop than eat!

WALLIS SIMPSON

✦

I feel sexy when I get out of the tub—your skin is fresh and you've put up your hair without looking.

SHANIA TWAIN

✦

She had the loaded handbag of someone who camps out and seldom goes home, or who imagines life must be full of emergencies.

MAVIS GALLANT

✦

I love color and I love to dress like a woman.

LISA GUERRERO

✦

I don't go out without makeup. I'm a woman, you know.

SHAKIRA

There are no ugly women, only lazy ones.

HELENA RUBINSTEIN

I will buy any crème, cosmetic, or elixir from a
woman with a European accent.

ERMA BOMBECK

Going hungry never bothered me—it
was having no clothes!

CHER

✦

Every best-dressed woman keeps some of her
gowns for years. She's learned that fashion-wisdom
is compounded of knowledge, taste, confidence,
and poise.

LORETTA YOUNG

✦

You'd be surprised how much it costs to
look this cheap.

DOLLY PARTON

I always say shopping is cheaper than a psychiatrist.

TAMMY FAYE MESSNER

✦

The only thing that separates us from the animals is our ability to accessorize.

OLYMPIA DUKAKIS

✦

Paint your nails in two tones—next time you get a French manicure, ask for lime green and pink, or red and gold, or black with orange tips! Get creative!

OLIVIA LAMONDE

✦

For your next office holiday party or power lunch, go vintage! Many higher-end vintage clothing stores sell dresses, suits, and blouses in like-new condition at a fraction of the cost of new designer clothing. These items are usually high quality and add flair to your wardrobe. Vintage clothing creates a classic and unique look.

TRINA ROBBINS

Use your favorite lotion in your hair! It tames the frizzies and scents your hair beautifully!

ALICE MARY ALVREZ

A purse with panache is a great way to update your wardrobe. Invest in four (practical) purses you absolutely love and alternate them on a regular basis. For a quick change of purses, keep your wallet, cell phone, keys, and favorite lipstick in a small makeup bag that can be transferred at the drop of a hat!

LIZA MINELLI

Jewelry is a quick and great way to add some pizzazz to your outfit; try sporting your favorite earrings and a dazzling necklace. Once a year, treat yourself and get all your jewelry professionally cleaned—your gems will sparkle like new!

CHER

I take Him shopping with me. I say, "Okay, Jesus, help me find a bargain."

TAMMY FAYE MESSNER

Forget diamonds, a girl's best friend is the
perfect-fitting dress!

AMANDA FORD

✦

Buy a collection of essential oils and make your
own fragrances and blends. Start with the basics,
like lavender, orange, and mint, and expand as you
experiment. You can customize your sheets and
laundry soap with your new scent. You can even
scent your household cleaner by adding a few drops
of lavender oil! Create your own signature scent!

RHIANNON MAHONEY

Owning Yourself

Nothing makes a woman more beautiful than the
belief that she is beautiful.

SOPHIA LOREN

We have to have faith in ourselves. I have never
met a woman who, deep down in her core, really
believes she has great legs. And if she suspects that
she might have great legs, then she's convinced
that she has a shrill voice and no neck.

CYNTHIA HEIMEL

Fashion trends may not last forever, but the photos will.

ALICE TURNER

Even the most beautiful couture looks shabby if you can't hold your head high and strike a good pose.

SANDRA COOR

I represent more the healthy, happy, curvy, strong woman. And that sounds much healthier to me than being eighty pounds and skinny as a bean.

HEIDI KLUM

Toughness doesn't have to come in a pinstripe suit.

SENATOR DIANNE FEINSTEIN

✦

Get really dressed up for work one day for no other reason than just "putting your best foot forward," in your best earrings, a stunning suit, or a pretty dress, and obviously, your favorite dressy shoes.

LARA STARR

We've come a long way. Power dressing now is designed to let the woman inside us come through.

DONNA KARAN

While clothes may not make the woman, they certainly have a strong effect on her self-confidence—which, I believe, does make the woman.

MARY KAY ASH

Vamp It Up

Being a sex symbol has to do with an attitude, not looks. Most men think it's looks, most women know otherwise.

KATHLEEN TURNER

A woman is no older than she looks.

ELIZABETH TAYLOR

It's no secret that I love a powerful yet slightly fragile woman such as Garbo, Lillian Gish, Bette Davis…that's where I get my inspirations from.

SIOBHAN FAHEY

Glamour is what I sell; it's my stock in trade.

MARLENE DIETRICH

There are various orders of beauty, causing men to make fools of themselves in various styles.

GEORGE ELIOT

Wear red! It is flattering on everyone and a great alternative to black.

RIRI

I don't know who invented high heels, but all women owe him a lot.

MARILYN MONROE

Sex appeal is fifty percent what you've got and fifty percent what people think you've got.

SOPHIA LOREN

✦

Scratch most feminists and underneath there is a woman who longs to be a sex object. The difference is that is not all she wants to be.

BETTY ROLLIN

Brainy Is Beautiful

Any girl can be glamorous. All you have to do is stand still and look stupid.

HEDY LAMARR

You don't have to signal a social conscience by looking like a frump. Lace knickers won't hasten the holocaust…and a mild interest in the length of hemlines doesn't necessarily disqualify you from reading *Das Kapital* and agreeing with every word.

ELIZABETH BIBESCO

You get out of fashion what you put into it.

LORETTA YOUNG

I'm not interested in age. People who tell me their age are silly. You're as old as you feel.

ELIZABETH ARDEN

If truth is beauty, how come no one has her hair done in a library?

LILY TOMLIN

I'm not obsessed by how I look or with being reed thin, but I do think that as a woman in my fifties, I have forty years ahead. Looking after yourself goes hand in hand with looking good.

LINDA EVANS

Don't buy clothes at the last minute, and try to decide what you are going to wear to an important meeting or a date night in advance. If possible, try the outfit on a few nights before the event and wear it around your apartment to make sure you are comfortable.

KATY PERRY

Elegance is refusal.

COCO CHANEL

I began wearing hats as a young lawyer because it helped me to establish my professional identity. Before that, whenever I was at a meeting, someone would ask me to get the coffee—they assumed I was a secretary.

CONGRESSWOMAN BELLA ABZUG

Give Your Old Clothes a Promotion

Donate your unworn professional clothing to www. dressforsuccess.org. This organization promotes economic independence for disadvantaged women by providing them with clothing they can wear to job interviews and to their place of work.

Chapter Four

With a Little Help from Your Friends, Family, and a Mentor or Two

We need friends. What would life be without them? Lonely, for one. What does friendship mean? Friends touch our hearts, enrich our lives, bolster our hopes, and forgive our ugly moments. They offer an outside perspective. They know us better than we know ourselves. True friends give sound advice and tell us the truth, even when it hurts. They listen to our woes and our joys and stand by us when no one else will.

The girl you met on the first day of second grade. Your mentor at work. The great aunt who swoops into town to take you to a fancy lunch just when you need it most. Friends who share passions or live just down the street. Through friends, we are connected by degrees to every other human being on the planet, so friendship really does bind the world together.

Even better, friends are free of charge. There are no legal ties to friendship, no contracts, usually not even a blood relationship (though being friends with your mom, sisters, or cousins has its own rewards). They are the people we choose to bond with—and they become our second family. Sometimes they're way more sane and likable than the one we're born into.

What about the dreaded fight with your best friend? It leaves you heartsick, and if you can't patch it up, you'll feel the ache for a long time to come. Take my advice and do what you can to make it better. Life's too short to live with regrets, and way too short to live without good friends. When I look back on fights with friends, I cringe at my own silly pride.

The only thing better than having a friend is *being* a friend. With friendship comes responsibility—the challenge of looking outside ourselves and investing in someone else's happiness. The greatest reward of friendship is helping your friends become their best in every way.

We don't always have to donate time and energy to other parts of the world. Sometimes help is needed much closer to home. Is a parent, sibling, spouse, or friend having a difficult time? Let them experience that loving feeling and help lift their spirits. Invite them to coffee or to dinner, surprise them with a simple gift, and take them somewhere they like. Lean forward and listen closely. Just hear them out, because listening is an act of love.

The Wonder of Friends

My true friends have always given me that supreme
proof of devotion, a spontaneous aversion to the
man I loved.

COLETTE

Time spent with friends is healing because we don't
perceive it as time. We just are.

GRACE MORTON

Trouble is like a sieve through which we sift our
acquaintances. Those too big to pass through are
our friends.

ARLENE FRANCIS

To be rich in friends is to be poor in nothing.

LILIAN WHITING

Each friend represents a world in us, a world
possibly not born until they arrive, and it is only by
this meeting that a new world is born.

ANAÏS NIN

A friend is someone who knows all about you and loves you anyway!

NANCY LAUREN FISH

✦

Though friendship is not quick to burn, it is explosive stuff.

MAY SARTON

✦

Walking with a friend in the dark is better than walking alone in the light.

HELEN KELLER

✦

The friend who holds your hand and says the wrong thing is made of dearer stuff than the one who stays away.

BARBARA KINGSOLVER

✦

Happiness is the comfortable companionship of friends.

PAM BROWN

Animals are such agreeable friends, they ask no
questions, they pass no criticism.

GEORGE ELIOT

✦

What's really important in life—friends,
friends, friends.

FANNIE FLAGG

✦

A friend is someone who reaches for your hand but
touches your heart.

KATHLEEN FROVE

Friends are like angels following you through life.

MARY ELLEN

My friends are my estate.

EMILY DICKINSON

✦

Never doubt that a small group of dedicated
people can make a difference. Indeed, it is the only
thing that ever has.

MARGARET MEAD

Life's truest happiness is found in friendships we make along the way.

LAUREN RUIZ

✦

A friend is someone who knows the song in your heart and can sing it back to you when you have forgotten the words.

DONNA ROBERTS

What Would We Do Without Them

Loneliness is the most terrible poverty.

MOTHER TERESA

The only true disability would be to go through life without friendship.

LAURA FORTH

✦

It seems to me that trying to live without friends is like milking a bear to get cream for your morning coffee. It is a whole lot of trouble, and then not worth much after you get it.

ZORA NEALE HURSTON

A friend is like a four-leaf clover, hard to find but lucky to have.

SAMANTHA ROSALES

CARE AND FEEDING

A friendship can weather most things and thrive in thin soil; but it needs a little mulch of letters and phone calls and small, silly presents every so often—just to save it from drying out completely.

PAM BROWN

Plant a seed of friendship—reap a bouquet of happiness.

LOIS L. KAUFMAN

There may not be a recipe for friendship, but that doesn't mean there are no rules.

BLANCHE HARDING

They call it "making friends" for a reason. It takes effort, and the right ingredients.

SANDRA GARRETT

A new friendship is like an unripened fruit—it may become either an orange or a lemon.

EMMA STACEY

If you judge people, you have no time to love them.

MOTHER TERESA

Silences make the real conversations between friends. Not the saying but the never needing to say is what counts.

MARGARET LEE RUNBECK

It takes a lot of courage to show your dreams to someone else.

ERMA BOMBECK

The sharing of joy, whether physical, emotional, psychic, or intellectual, forms a bridge between the sharers which can be the basis for understanding much of what is not shared between them, and lessens the threat of their difference.

AUDRE LORDE

The only thing to do is to hug one's friends tight
and do one's job.

EDITH WHARTON

For women, talk is the glue that holds relationships
together; it creates connections between people
and a sense of community.

DEBORAH FARMER

Count your joys instead of your woes; count your
friends instead of your foes.

IRISH PROVERB

Strangers are just friends waiting to happen!

WENDY WENTWORTH

✦

Make new friends and keep the old; one is silver
and the other is gold.

GIRL SCOUT MOTTO

We are each other's magnitude and bond.
GWENDOLYN BROOKS

✦

"Stay" is a charming word in a friend's vocabulary.
LOUISA MAY ALCOTT

Connection

Friendship is the golden ribbon that ties the
world together.
KRISTINA KENTIGLAN

I am treating you as my friend, asking you to share
my present minuses in the hope I can ask you to
share my future pluses.
KATHERINE MANSFIELD

✦

Two may talk together under the same roof for
many years, yet never really meet; and two others
at first speech are old friends.
MARY CATHERWOOD

Though our communication wanes at times of absence, I'm aware of a strength that emanates in the background.

CLAUDETTE RENNER

In loneliness, in sickness, in confusion—the mere knowledge of friendship makes it possible to endure, even if the friend is powerless to help. It is enough that they exist.

PAM BROWN

Ah, how good it feels…the hand of an old friend.

MARY ENGELBREIT

I don't want to lose this happy space where I have found someone who is smart and easy and doesn't bother to check her diary when we arrange to meet.

JEANETTE WINTERSON

✦

There is magic in long-distance friendships. They let you relate to other human beings in a way that goes beyond being physically together and is often more profound.

DIANA CORTES

There is no distance too great between friends, for love gives wings to the heart.

ELIZABETH E. KOEHLER

Some people go to priests; others to poetry; I to my friends.

VIRGINIA WOOLF

Giving

You never lose by loving. You always lose by holding back.

BARBARA DE ANGELIS

If we would build on a sure foundation in friendship, we must love friends for their own sake rather than our own.

CHARLOTTE BRONTË

I don't get women who pick fights with their friends.
It's not like you get to kiss and make up afterwards.
Play those games with your lover if you have to, but
don't toy with a good friendship.

MARCIA BOND

We all need friends with whom we can speak of our
deepest concerns, and who do not fear to speak
the truth in love to us.

REV. MARGARET GUENTHER

The finest kind of friendship is between two
people who expect a great deal of each other, but
never ask it.

SYLVIA BREMER

✦

Constant use will not wear ragged the fabric
of friendship.

DOROTHY PARKER

✦

The best time to make friends is before you
need them.

ETHEL BARRYMORE

It's important to our friends to believe that we are unreservedly frank with them, and important to the friendship that we are not.

MIGNON MCLAUGHLIN

Send a thank you note to a good friend, a relative, or coworker "just because" and let them know what you appreciate about them. This "attitude of gratitude" will take you far in your life and will come back to you many times over.

MARY JANE RYAN

A real friend is one who walks in when the rest of the world walks out.

JENNIFER ANISTON

Friendship with oneself is all-important, because without it, one cannot be friends with anybody else in the world.

ELEANOR ROOSEVELT

✦

I've always believed that one woman's success can only help another woman's success.

GLORIA VANDERBILT

We cherish our friends not for their ability to amuse
us, but for ours to amuse them.

EVELYN WAUGH

A good friend brings out the best in everybody!

MIMI COOKE

Growing

The most beautiful discovery that true friends
can make is that you can grow separately without
growing apart.

ELIZABETH FOLEY

All you'll get from strangers is surface pleasantry
or indifference. Only someone who loves you will
criticize you.

JUDITH CRIST

Four be the things I am wiser to know: Idleness,
sorrow, a friend, and a foe.

DOROTHY PARKER

No person is your friend who demands your silence,
or denies your right to grow.

ALICE WALKER

Parents start you off on life but friends
get you through it.

DEE CHOU

I can trust my friends. These people force me to
examine, encourage me to grow.

CHER

✦

It is the friends you call up at 4 a.m. that matter.

MARLENE DIETRICH

Don't Be Judgmental:

Be Kind Just Because You Can

It's easy to judge others for their actions and take for granted those we love or those we meet in chance encounters. We sometimes get so caught up in our busyness that we forget others are busy too, they have rough days just like us, and they benefit from our kindnesses just as we do from theirs. Go out of your way to smile at strangers, say good morning, say thank you, give a compliment, and listen attentively to someone who needs your ear. Do it because you can, because it feels great, because it makes someone else feel good. Don't worry about a subsequent thank you; let a thank you be a beautiful perk, rather than an expectation.

Chapter Five
Treat Yourself Well: Hard Work Deserves Reward

Think about how you can create little moments of happiness for others. Helping a friend plant her garden, buying an extra coffee for your coworker, paying the toll for the car behind you on the bridge, even taking your kids to a movie. All those little things can add up to *big* joy.

Now apply that same thinking to yourself. Try soaking your feet, having a facial, treating yourself to dinner. Or even going beyond the mundane to splurge on a real vacation. Vacations are really important. A weekend on the beach can erase a month of city tension. And you can learn new things, work through problems, and strengthen relationships at turbo speeds in the parallel vacation universe. Go on, give it a try. Make a commitment to pamper yourself a little on the way to realizing your dreams.

You Deserve It

I have an everyday religion that works for me. Love yourself first, and everything else falls into line.

LUCILLE BALL

✦

To be a saint does not exclude fine dresses nor a beautiful house.

KATHERINE TYNAN HINKSON

✦

Chocolate has iron in it. Surely that's why I like it so much.

ERIN YOUNG

✦

Birds sing after a storm; why shouldn't people feel as free to delight in whatever remains to them?

ROSE FITZGERALD KENNEDY

As women, we are taught to fear our own desires much more than men. Anything we want, we are told, should be considered suspect…. While it is wise to carefully examine what we want and what we need, wanting in itself should not be so feared.

ALANA PRICE

If you always do what interests you, then at least one person is pleased.

KATHARINE HEPBURN

I have low self-esteem, but I express it the healthy way…by eating a box of Double-Stuff Oreos.

MIRANDA (CYNTHIA NIXON), *SEX AND THE CITY*

Money earned with pains should be spent with pleasure.

CHINESE PROVERB

Pleasure that isn't paid for is as insipid as everything else that's free.

ANITA LOOS

We can each define ambition and progress for ourselves. The goal is to work toward a world where expectations are not set by the stereotypes that hold us back, but by our personal passion, talents, and interests.

SHERYL SANDBERG

Without leaps of imagination or dreaming, we lose the excitement of possibilities. Dreaming, after all, is a form of planning.

GLORIA STEINEM

Don't Wait

Life is uncertain. Eat desserts first.

MARGIE LAPANJA

Our best gifts to ourselves may be few, but that doesn't mean they have to be far between.

DELILAH CARR

Seize the moment. Remember all those women on the Titanic who waved off the dessert cart.

ERMA BOMBECK

✦

You have to treat yourself every once in a while, get to the fun stuff!

HEIDI KLUM

✦

The essence of pleasure is spontaneity.

GERMAINE GREER

✦

While many fantasies are best left to the realm of the imagination, some must be fulfilled if we are to be healthy, growing individuals.

AMANDA BENNET

✦

It is only possible to live happily-ever-after on a day-to-day basis.

MARGARET THATCHER

Never let your senses become dulled to your life.
They are your only links to the world around you.

JUSTINE THOREAU

✦

This very moment is a seed from which the flowers
of tomorrow's happiness grow.

MARGARET LINDSEY

✦

I believe in dreams, not just the kind we have at
night. I think that if we hang on to them, they
come true.

DANIELLE STEEL

✦

Life is to be lived.

KATHARINE HEPBURN

The Best Things in Life (and Some Are Free!)

I love luxury. And luxury lies not in richness and ornateness but in the absence of vulgarity.

COCO CHANEL

Food is, delightfully, an area of licensed sensuality, of physical delight, which will, with luck and enduring taste buds, last our life long.

ANTONIA TILL

No entertainment is so cheap as reading, nor any pleasure so lasting.

MARY WORTLEY MONTAGU

Fragrance can have a great effect on our well-being, triggering happy memories or unlocking our sensuality. Indulge in some new oils, candles, or perfumes and enjoy the results.

NANCY KLINE

Call your best friend for no other reason than just to catch up—indulge in laughs, a quick catch-up, and the beauty of friendship.

LEIGH STONE

✦

Music melts all the separate parts of our bodies together.

ANAÏS NIN

Over-the-Top Indulgence

It is impossible to overdo luxury.

FRENCH PROVERB

We owe something to extravagance, for thrift and adventure seldom go hand in hand.

JENNIE JEROME CHURCHILL

We must deprogram ourselves from the belief that all indulgence is sinful. Only excess is sinful.

YOLANDA BROOKS

Life itself is the proper binge.

JULIA CHILD

Art may be one of humankind's biggest indulgences, but it's also basic to our survival.

MARYA WHITBECK

Take care of the luxuries and the necessities will take care of themselves.

DOROTHY PARKER

To be overcome by the fragrance of flowers is a delectable form of defeat.

BEVERLY NICHOLS

Try This

Eat outdoors. Enjoy an entire dinner service in the backyard, or even on a small balcony. If you don't have outdoor space, head for the park. Use real silverware and cloth napkins. Indulge!

BELINDA DECAMP

Go for a walk in the rain.

CYNTHIA MACGREGOR

✦

Make your bedroom a sensuous place for refuge.
Do your work somewhere else in the house, and
decorate with your favorite colors and textures. It
should be your own special luxurious hideaway.

KATHRYN LAMONT

✦

Those who allow their day to pass by without
practicing generosity and enjoying life's pleasures
are like a blacksmith's bellows: they breathe but
do not live.

PROVERB

When I thought I had seen it all, I went for a ride
in a hot air balloon. The perspective renewed my
sense of awe in the world around me!

PATTY HELMS

Treat yourself to the sweet joy of dreaming
of beautiful things, a fabulous job, a
fulfilling relationship.

JUDY FORD

Every time I get a paycheck, I take a few dollars from it and set them aside for myself. That way, I have a small fund for when I see that perfect pair of pumps, without having to pump my credit card.

BETHANY FLEMING

Live nutty. Just occasionally. Just once in a while and see what happens. It brightens up your day.

PAT GURITZ

Whip up an easy batch of your own bath salts. Inexpensive Epsom salts from the pharmacy will do; for a real treat, mix them with sea salt. Toss them into a Ziploc bag and add a few drops of your favorite essential oil. Shake the baggie until the oil is distributed throughout, and then draw yourself a hot bath!

FRANCIS L. BAG

Give yourself a scalp massage the next time you wash your hair.

DOLLY WHITTIER

Paint a room in your house or apartment a color
you love—fiery red, bright blue, or lavishing
lavender—and enjoy the new ambiance.

CERRIDWEN GREENLEAF

Give yourself a break from cooking tonight; instead,
have dinner delivered and enjoy your additional
free time.

JENNIFER LEWIS

Far away there in the sunshine are my highest
aspirations. I may not reach them, but I can look
up and see their beauty, believe in them, and try to
follow where they lead.

LOUISA MAY ALCOTT

Simple Pleasures

I have a simple philosophy: Fill what's empty. Empty
what's full. Scratch where it itches.

ALICE ROOSEVELT LONGWORTH

It's an indulgence to sit in a room and discuss your
beliefs as if they were a juicy piece of gossip.

LILLIAN HELLMAN

Life in the country teaches one that the really
stimulating things are the quiet, natural things....
The scent of grass is more luxurious than the most
expensive perfume.

BEVERLEY NICHOLS

Real luxury is time and opportunity to read
for pleasure.

JANE BRODY

To me, a lush carpet of pine needles or spongy
grass is more welcome than the most luxurious
Persian rug.

HELEN KELLER

✦

Start a garden and plant it with only your favorite
seasonal flowers. Grow your own special outdoor
retreat, even if it's only a window box.

CYNTHIA KINGSTON

What do I want to take home from my summer vacation? Time. The wonderful luxury of being at rest. The days when you shut down…and let life simply wander.

ELLEN GOODMAN

Buying is a profound pleasure.

SIMONE DE BEAUVOIR

If one could be friendly with women, what a pleasure—the relationship so secret and private compared with relations with men.

VIRGINIA WOOLF

Museums and art stores are also sources of pleasure and inspiration…it is true that I derive genuine pleasure from touch.

HELEN KELLER

God made all pleasures innocent.

CAROLINE NORTON

No Strings Attached

Write down the things that someone has given you, with no strings attached, for which you are grateful. It can be an old sofa, some sound advice, or a lift to the airport. Now list ten things that you would like to give someone yourself, and see how many of those things you can cross off in a week.

Examples:

Drive a friend to the airport

Carry groceries for an elder

Babysit for a relative

Buy a friend a cup of coffee

Volunteer at a soup kitchen

Weed an older neighbor's garden

Take fresh-out-of-the-oven doughnuts to a senior center

and hang out

CHAPTER SIX
Living Your Best Life Every Day

Take stock of your day-to-day life. Are you giving to others in your community, or are things a little out of balance where your work and your immediate family get 99 percent of what you offer the world? You can change that in one day by reconnecting to your dreams. What were your dreams when you were a child? We're all striving to make the most of what we've got; we all want better lives. But sometimes this desire becomes twisted, and we start to think that if only we had more money, or different circumstances, or the grass was just a little greener, our lives would be perfect. Well, I am here to attest that perfect is boring⬛and life should be anything but boring. And while more and better stuff might be fun for a while, the real fun starts when we embrace the intangibles. The ingredients of a well-lived life are yours for the choosing: openness, strength, courage, dignity, responsibility, passion, positivity, energy, beauty, and whatever else you fancy.

It's time to take control of your destiny. Time to merge your inner child's enthusiasm with your adult experience. Believe you can live beyond your wildest dreams, voice your desires and act on them, and reap the benefits of a life lived to the hilt!

Uncover Your Soul's Purpose

When we are on track, living close to the things we deem important—the things we value—we feel happier. This isn't flash happiness, it isn't the kind that lasts for a few minutes when we get a new toy or enjoy a concert. This is the kind that lingers in the background of our lives, the kind that, even in moments of sadness or frustration, never completely disappears, because if we are living a values-based life, we are also living with meaning and purpose.

POLLY CAMPBELL

A bird doesn't sing because it has an answer, it sings because it has a song.

MAYA ANGELOU

The most important thing you will ever do is become who you were meant to be. Blossom into yourself.

LISA HAMMOND

Invest in the human soul. Who knows, it might be a diamond in the rough.

MARY MCLEOD BETHUNE

Life is what we make it, always has been, always will be.

GRANDMA MOSES

Don't be afraid your life will end; be afraid that it will never begin.

GRACE HANSEN

You don't get to choose how you're going to die, or when. You can only decide how you're going to live now.

JOAN BAEZ

I have always had a dread of becoming a passenger in life.

MARGARET II, QUEEN OF DENMARK

In great moments, life seems neither right nor wrong, but something greater; it seems inevitable.

MARGARET SHERWOOD

You are all you will ever have for certain.

JUNE HAVOC

Finding your passion is about connecting the dots between your head and your heart.

MARIA MARSALA

People are like stained glass windows. They sparkle and shine when the sun is out, but when the darkness sets in, their true beauty is revealed only if there is light from within.

ELIZABETH KÜBLER-ROSS

I have learned not to worry about love, but to honor its coming with all my heart.

ALICE WALKER

No trumpets sound when the important
decisions of our lives are made. Destiny is made
known silently.

AGNES DE MILLE

Some women go through life turning on lamps in
the evening. Others are themselves a light.

HELEN PERKES

The Ingredients of a Wonderful Life

The kind of beauty I want most is the hard-
to-get kind that comes from within: strength,
courage, dignity.

RUBY DEE

Life is a mystery as deep as ever death can be.

MARY MAPES DODGE

Eating is not merely a material pleasure. Eating well gives a spectacular joy to life and contributes immensely to good will and happy companionship. It is of great importance to the morale.

ELSA SCHIAPARELLI

Good communication is just as stimulating as black coffee, and just as hard to sleep after.

ANNE MORROW LINDBERGH

The point is not to pay back kindness but to pass it on.

JULIA ALVAREZ

The things we truly love stay with us always, locked in our hearts as long as life remains.

JOSEPHINE BAKER

The only thing that makes life possible is permanent, intolerable uncertainty; not knowing what comes next.

URSULA K. LE GUIN

I'm not happy, I'm cheerful. There's a difference. A happy woman has no cares at all. a cheerful woman has cares but has learned how to deal with them.

BEVERLY SILLS

The universe is made of stories, not of atoms.

MURIEL RUKEYSER

No one has a right to consume happiness without producing it.

HELEN KELLER

Desire, ask, believe, receive.

STELLA TERRILL MANN

Live as if you like yourself, and it may happen.

MARGE PIERCY

Choice is all we have. Choice is all we need.

KAREN CASEY

Learn to trust your own judgment, learn inner independence, learn to trust that time will sort good from bad—including your own bad.

DORIS LESSING

✦

The cure for boredom is curiosity. There is no cure for curiosity.

ELLEN PARR

✦

Without an open-minded mind, you can never be a great success.

MARTHA STEWART

✦

Grace, growth, and gratitude: these are my highest aspirations.

GLORIA ARLISS

✦

"Yes" is contagious on a subliminal level. It affects everything you do.

SARK

Happily, love is a pleasant emotion and thrives as
well in stables as in palaces.

DIANE ACKERMAN

Life is better than death, I believe, if only because it
is less boring, and because it has fresh peaches in it.

ALICE WALKER

Count on Your Own Character

Don't compromise yourself. You are all you've got.

JANIS JOPLIN

Civilization is a method of living and an attitude of
equal respect for all people.

JANE ADDAMS

As long as you keep a person down, some part of
you has to be down there to hold him down, so it
means you cannot soar as you otherwise might.

MARIAN ANDERSON

I would rather die a meaningful death than live a meaningless life.

CORAZON AQUINO

✦

Character builds slowly, but it can be torn down with incredible swiftness.

FAITH BALDWIN

✦

You can stand tall without standing on someone. You can be a victor without having victims.

HARRIET WOODS

✦

We cannot afford not to fight for growth and understanding, even when it is painful, as it is bound to be.

MAY SARTON

✦

Self-respect cannot be hunted…. It comes to us when we are alone, in quiet moments, in quiet places, when we suddenly realize that, knowing the good, we have done it; knowing the beautiful, we have served it; knowing the truth, we have spoken it.

WHITNEY GRISWOLD

If you can't change your fate, change your attitude.

AMY TAN

The willingness to accept responsibility for one's own life is the source from which self-respect springs.

JOAN DIDION

✦

My recipe for life is not being afraid of myself, afraid of what I think, or of my opinions.

EARTHA KITT

Live in Your Prime All the Time

The hardest years are those between ten and seventy.

HELEN HAYES

The history of all times, and of today especially, teaches that…women will be forgotten if they forget to think about themselves.

LOUISE OTTO

Strive for Five—try to learn five new words a week; it keeps your brain active and helps your memory skills. Also, a wild woman with a very large vocabulary is a very potent combination.

AUTUMN STEPHENS

So much has been said and sung of beautiful young girls, why doesn't somebody wake up to the beauty of old women?

HARRIET BEECHER STOWE

One's prime is elusive. You little girls, when you grow up, must be on the alert to recognize your prime at whatever time of your life it may occur.

MURIEL SPARK

The wisdom acquired with the passage of time is a useless gift unless you share it.

ESTHER WILLIAMS

I hope when this life is over, people will say of me, "She lived, she laughed, she loved with all that she was." Consider what you want people to remember of you and live accordingly.

BARB ROGERS

I learned a woman is never an old woman.

JONI MITCHELL

If we had no winter, the spring would not be so pleasant; if we did not sometimes taste of adversity, prosperity would not be so welcome.

ANNE BRADSTREET

Age is something that doesn't matter, unless you are a cheese.

BILLIE BURKE

What a wonderful life I've had! I only wish I'd realized it sooner.

COLETTE

I am beautiful as I am. I am the shape that was gifted. My breasts are no longer perky and upright like when I was a teenager. My hips are wider than those of a fashion model. For this I am glad, for these are the signs of a life lived.

CINDY OLSEN

What is amazing for a woman of my age is that I change as the world is changing—and changing very, very fast. I don't think my mother had that opportunity to change.

JEANNE MOREAU

The secret of staying young is to live honestly, eat slowly, and lie about your age.

LUCILLE BALL

Grow to Learn, Learn to Grow

I don't want to get to the end of my life and find
that I lived just the length of it. I want to have lived
the width of it as well.

DIANE ACKERMAN

A really strong woman accepts the war she went
through and is ennobled by her scars.

CARLY SIMON

Fortunately, psychoanalysis is not the only way to
resolve inner conflicts. Life itself remains a very
effective therapist.

KAREN HORNEY

✦

You must learn day by day, year by year, to broaden
your horizon. The more things you love, the more
you are interested in, the more you enjoy, the more
you are indignant about, the more you have left
when anything happens.

ETHEL BARRYMORE

People don't live nowadays; they get about ten
percent out of life.

ISADORA DUNCAN

✦

Happiness must be cultivated. It is like character. It
is not a thing to be safely let alone for a moment, or
it will run to weeds.

ELIZABETH STUART PHELPS

✦

One is not born a woman, one becomes one.

SIMONE DE BEAUVOIR

✦

You need only claim the events of your life to make
yourself yours. When you truly possess all that you
have been and done, which may take some time,
you are fierce with reality.

FLORIDA SCOTT MAXWELL

If we don't change, we don't grow. If we don't
grow, we are not really living. Growth demands a
temporary surrender of security.

GAIL SHEEHY

Adventure is worthwhile in itself.

AMELIA EARHART

At the moment you are most in awe of all there is
about life that you don't understand, you are closer
to understanding it all than at any other time.

JANE WAGNER

Learn to get in touch with the silence within yourself
and know that everything has a purpose. There
are no mistakes, no coincidences, all events are
blessings given to us to learn from.

ELIZABETH KÜBLER-ROSS

Mistakes are part of the dues one pays for a full life.

SOPHIA LOREN

Random acts of kindness—simple acts of generosity—are not only nice for other people, but they actually are healthy for you physically as well as spiritually. They reduce levels of stress hormones. So go ahead and make yourself and others happy today!

MARY RUSKIN

Life engenders life. Energy creates energy. It is by spending oneself that one becomes rich.

SARAH BERNHARDT

Take Time to Check in With Yourself Unplug
(and Recharge!)

Forego using technological devices today. Texting your friend, watching your favorite show, checking your email—all can wait until tomorrow! Turn off your devices and turn on your senses! Read a book, cook a meal, and enjoy the outdoors by taking a walk or tending to your garden. Technology distracts us from the real world; it occupies our attention with game applications, chat rooms, social media websites, commercials, and so on. Want to know what's going on in the news? Read a newspaper. Be aware of the here and now by finding activities that don't require electricity or a battery. Make your own entertainment!

Chapter Seven

Daring Greatly: Making Sure Your Creativity and Ideas Count

This is your life, only you can truly control your choices, and choosing to dare is the best way to achieve being good to yourself as well as to the world. Here are some suggestions for how you can ensure simple daring in your life:

- Be the best you can be by your own standards

- Surround yourself with people who inspire you and make you feel good

- Focus on what you have, not what you lack

- Remember that optimism trumps pessimism every time!

- Smile often and genuinely

- Be honest, both to yourself and to others

- Help others

- Embrace your past, live in the present, and look forward to what is yet to come

- Make radical self-belief your motto. BELIEVE!

Think about what makes life worth living—risk, daring, courage, and growth.

Some people seem to have a knack for it. We say they march to their own drum; we're wowed by their resilience in the face of criticism and adversity. If you are one of those people, it's time to share your secrets with the rest of us and be a cheerleader for the timid among us. And if you're not one of those people yet, remember that we can all choose to put ourselves on the line as we go after our dreams, and we can always try to use our mistakes as lessons on the road to success. Decide that what you want is more important than your fear of getting it, and there is no stopping you. Nothing ventured, nothing gained. Life's an adventure, so venture forth and reach for your dreams!

*I*NNER *S*TRENGTH

A sheltered life can be a daring life as well. For all
serious daring starts from within.

EUDORA WELTY

I never realized until lately that women were
supposed to be the inferior sex.

KATHARINE HEPBURN

It's better to be a lion for a day than a sheep
all your life.

SISTER ELIZABETH KENNY

Our strength is often composed of the weakness
we're damned if we're going to show.

MIGNON MCLAUGHLIN

Men are taught to apologize for their weaknesses,
women for their strengths.

LOIS WYSE

We women talk too much, nevertheless, we only say half of what we know.

NANCY ASTOR

✦

There is a growing strength in women, but it is in the forehead, not in the forearm.

BEVERLY SILLS

I've been through it all, baby. I'm mother courage.

ELIZABETH TAYLOR

✦

More than anything, I think as our country matures, we recognize that women deserve to be treated with respect and dignity.

BARBARA BOXER

✦

A woman is like a tea bag—you can't tell how strong she is until you put her in hot water.

ELEANOR ROOSEVELT

Always be a first-rate version of yourself, instead of
a second-rate version of somebody else.

JUDY GARLAND

Remember, no one can make you feel inferior
without your consent.

ELEANOR ROOSEVELT

✦

It's sexy to be competent.

LETTY COTTIN POGREBIN

✦

If you do things well, do them better. Be daring, be
first, be different, be just.

ANITA RODDICK

✦

You were once wild here. Don't let them tame you.

ISADORA DUNCAN

✦

I'm tough, ambitious, and I know exactly what I want.

MADONNA

I think that women making no apology for being
women is very refreshing.

DREW BARRYMORE

✦

Real power is when you are doing exactly what you
are supposed to be doing the best it can be done.

OPRAH WINFREY

Shaking Things Up

If you think you are too small to be effective, you
have never been in bed with a mosquito.

BETTY REESE

We lift our voices as one; let all know, we are here,
and we intend to stay!

NANCY FREDERICK

Cautious, careful people always casting about to preserve their reputation or social standards never can bring about reform. Those who are really in earnest are willing to be anything or nothing in the world's estimation…and bear the consequences.

SUSAN B. ANTHONY

✦

We've chosen the path to equality, don't let them turn us around.

GERALDINE FERRARO

✦

If particular care and attention are not paid to the ladies, we are determined to foment a rebellion, and will not hold ourselves bound by any laws in which we have no voice or representation.

ABIGAIL ADAMS

✦

Justice is better than chivalry if we cannot have both.

ALICE STONE BLACKWELL

✦

I am in the world to change the world.

MURIEL RUKEYSER

I believe in a lively disrespect for most forms
of authority.

RITA MAE BROWN

✦

I prefer liberty to chains of diamonds.

LADY MARY WORTLEY MONTAGU

✦

Women belong in the house…and the Senate.

ANN RICHARDS

✦

What is enough? Enough is when somebody says,
'Get me the best people you can find' and nobody
notices when half of them turn out to be women.

LOUISE RENNE

✦

You can't get swept off your feet if you are sitting
down. Stand up and be noticed!

CLAIRE CAMDEN

✦

Men have always been afraid that women could get
along without them.

MARGARET MEAD

It's been a lot of fun making the revolution.

BETTY FRIEDAN

✦

I'll not listen to reason. Reason always means what someone else has got to say.

ELIZABETH GASKILL

Be a Bad Girl in a Good Way

Good girls go to heaven, bad girls go everywhere.

HELEN GURLEY BROWN

✦

Well-behaved women rarely make history.

LAUREL THATCHER ULRICH

✦

I do not want people to be agreeable, as it saves me the trouble of liking them.

JANE AUSTEN

Only good girls keep diaries. Bad girls don't
have time.

TALLULAH BANKHEAD

✦

When the sun comes up, I have morals again.

ELAYNE BOOSLER

✦

A woman can look both moral and exciting…if she
also looks as if it was quite a struggle.

EDNA FERBER

✦

Rules are for people who don't know how to get
around them.

TORI HARRISON

✦

I have too many fantasies to be a housewife. I guess
I am a fantasy.

MARILYN MONROE

One wonders what would happen in a society in
which there were no rules to break. Doubtless
everyone would quickly die of boredom.

SUSAN HOWITCH

I am not eccentric. It's just that I am more alive than
most people. I am an unpopular electric eel set in a
pond of goldfish.

DAME EDITH SITWELL

Women are the real architects of society.

HARRIET BEECHER STOWE

I'm extraordinarily patient provided I can get my
own way in the end.

MARGARET THATCHER

I've always taken risks, and never worried what the
world might really think of me.

CHER

I can, therefore I am.

SIMONE WEIL

✦

Some say the glass is half empty, some say the glass is half full; I say, are you going to drink that?

LISA CLAYMEN

✦

If I had to live my life again, I'd make the same mistakes, only sooner.

TALLULAH BANKHEAD

✦

Until you lose your reputation, you never realize what a burden it was or what freedom really is.

MARGARET MITCHELL

𝓕acing 𝓒hallenges

I'm not afraid of storms, for I'm learning to sail my ship.

LOUISA MAY ALCOTT

You can't be brave if you've only had wonderful things happen to you.

MARY TYLER MOORE

Remember that fear is something learned. None of us are born afraid.

MARY STANYAN

Whatever women do they must do twice as well as men to be thought half as good. Luckily, this is not difficult.

CHARLOTTE WHITTON

If you want anything said, ask a man. If you want something done, ask a woman.

MARGARET THATCHER

The naked truth is always better than the best-dressed lie.

ANN LANDERS

If it's a woman, it's caustic; if it's a man,
it's authoritative.

BARBARA WALTERS

If Rosa Parks had taken a poll before she sat down
on that bus in Montgomery, she'd still be standing.

MARY FRANCES BERRY

I once complained to my father that I didn't seem
to be able to do things the same way other people
did. Dad's advice? 'Margo, don't be a sheep.
People hate sheep. They eat sheep.'

MARGO KAUFMAN

✦

Speak up for yourself, or you'll end up a rug.

MAE WEST

✦

And the trouble is, if you don't risk anything,
you risk more.

ERICA JONG

Unleash Your Desire and Reach for Your Stars

It is our choices…that show what we truly are, far more than our abilities.

J.K. ROWLING

✦

When you have a dream, you've got to grab it and never let it go.

CAROL BURNETT

✦

I think the key is for women not to set any limits.

MARTINA NAVRATILOVA

✦

There are no dangerous thoughts; thinking itself is dangerous.

HANNAH ARENDT

Truth is always exciting. Speak it, then; life is dull without it.

PEARL S. BUCK

Be bold. If you're going to make an error, make a doozy, and don't be afraid to hit the ball.

BILLIE JEAN KING

Be bold in what you stand for and careful what you fall for.

RUTH BOORSTIN

To tell a woman everything she may not do is to tell her what she can do.

UNKNOWN

You may be imperious, but the effect is always spoiled when you apologize.

KAREN WILLIAMS

Real women don't have flushes, they have
power surges.

SANDRA CABOT

✦

When you believe in your dreams you are able to
fight for them.

CECILY BARRY

✦

All good fortune is a gift of the gods, and you don't
win the favor of the ancient gods by being good,
but by being bold.

ANITA BROOKNER

✦

The thing women have yet to learn is nobody gives
you power. You just take it.

ROSEANNE BARR

✦

If you don't act as if your name were on the door,
it never will be.

PATRICIA FRIPP

It's hard to be free, but when it works, it is
sure worth it.

JANIS JOPLIN

✦

Bite off more than you can chew, then chew it.

ELLA WILLIAMS

✦

The most effective way to do it, is to do it.

AMELIA EARHART

✦

Life shrinks or expands in proportion to
one's courage.

ANAÏS NIN

Catch People Doing Something Right

(and Make Sure They Know It!)

During stressful times or difficult transitions, our natural tendency is often to contract and grow rigid. In this mindset, we seem to only be able to focus on the negatives. We think about the despair and torment of the death of a loved one, but not the wonderful moments spent together. We think of the heartbreak of a relationship ending, but not of the exhilaration and freedom of being unattached. We might even scold our loved ones, our friends, or our coworkers for something minor or insignificant when we wallow in such negativity. But it is in these moments specifically that gratitude can be used to alter this way of thinking.

Finding positives and accentuating them is the easiest way to turn those proverbial frowns upside down and gray skies back to blue. Try catching someone doing something right for a change, not something wrong. Giving praise for a job well done lifts all parties involved and is the easiest—and perhaps best—way to say "Thank you" without actually having to say it.

CHAPTER EIGHT
Women Make All the Difference at Work

Instead of writing up and crossing things off of your to-do list or a "bucket list," create a "life list." Let your hopes, dreams, fears, and thoughts spill out of you and onto this list. Next to each entry, write down how that emotion or fear makes you feel—does it hold you back or empower you? This task will put you on the road to self-discovery. Knowing who you are is important in order to have relationships with others. Know thyself. And use this knowledge to up your effectiveness.

I've gotten into reading biographies and autobiographies of people whose lives and work inspire me. I've noticed that even in the case of the "overnight successes," you have to get at least halfway through the book of someone's life story before their hard work starts to pay off in any substantial way. I'm talking chapter after chapter of working for no recognition, no pay, and no glory; years or even decades of disappointments, detours, and being down in the dumps. But these people struggle through; some even find joy in the adversity. And somewhere in my reading, I think, "Right, of course!"

Pay, glory, and recognition are all great, but they aren't real motivators. If that's all you're working toward, you're probably never going to get there. Doing what you love and loving what you do is the real point. Then all that other stuff can be icing on the cake if and when it comes around. And even if you never get the kudos you deserve, you'll hardly notice as you chug along, reaping the rewards of a challenging, interesting career.

Dream up a goal, make a plan, and stay present in the moment as you work it out. Evaluate yourself and those around you honestly as you go, and keep the bigger picture in the forefront of your mind. You're going to have to think up new ways to work around obstacles, and you're going to have to battle some drudgery. That might be the hardest part. One way is to keep a reminder of your goals close at hand—a picture, a poem, a sketch—and look at it to help motivate you through the boring stuff. Put your nose to the grindstone, and watch as your worries fall away. Get your hands a little dirty and you'll be well on your way to being the best you can be.

Work As if It's Fulfilling

Work itself is the reward. If I choose challenging work, it will pay me back with interest.... This attempt for excellence is what sustains the most well-lived and satisfying, successful lives.

MERYL STREEP

People think at the end of the day that a man is the only answer [to fulfillment]. Actually, a job is better for me.

DIANA, PRINCESS OF WALES

Nothing gratifies one more than to be admired for doing what one likes.

DOROTHY L. SAYERS

I've never been a fan of work as it's usually defined by other people. But when I learned how to define it for myself, I realized that it actually can be as fulfilling as I'd always hoped.

BELINDA CASSIDY

Look at a day when you are supremely satisfied at the end of it. it's not a day when you lounge around doing nothing; it's when you've had everything to do, and you've done it.

MARGARET THATCHER

Work won't always make your heart sing. But when it does, it's one of the best feelings there is.

AMY PORTER

To follow without halt, one aim; there is the secret of success. And success? What is it? I do not find it in the applause of the theater; it lies rather in the satisfaction of accomplishment.

ANNA PAVLOVA

✦

Laziness may appear attractive, but work gives satisfaction.

ANNE FRANK

I look back on my life like a good day's work; it was done and I am satisfied with it.

GRANDMA MOSES

What we really want to do is what we are really meant to do. When we do what we are meant to do, money comes to us, doors open for us, we feel useful, and the work we do feels like play to us.

JULIA CAMERON

You are not in business to be popular.

KIRSTIE ALLEY

The most popular labor-saving device is still money.

PHYLLIS GEORGE

Work is the world's easiest escape from boredom and the only surefire road to success.

MARABEL MORGAN

The ability to control one's own destiny…comes from constant hard work and courage.

MAYA ANGELOU

To fulfill a dream, to be allowed to sweat over lonely labor, to be given a chance to create, is the meat and potatoes of life. The money is the gravy.

BETTE DAVIS

Measure not the work until the day's out and the labor is done.

ELIZABETH BARRETT BROWNING

Women hold up half the sky.

CHINESE PROVERB

Instead of thinking about where you are, think about where you want to be. It takes twenty years of hard work to become an overnight success.

DIANA RANKIN

What I know is, is that if you do work that you love,
and the work fulfills you, the rest will come.

OPRAH WINFREY

Find Your Balance

You cannot be really first-rate at your work if your
work is all you are.

ANNA QUINDLEN

I believe you are your work. Don't trade the stuff of
your life, time, for nothing more than dollars. That's
a rotten bargain.

RITA MAE BROWN

Take your work seriously, but never yourself.

MARGOT FONTEYN

Any woman who has a career and a family automatically develops something in the way of two personalities, like two sides of a dollar bill, each different in design…. Her problem is to keep one from draining the life from the other.

IVY BAKER PRIEST

✦

A human being must have occupation if he or she is not to become a nuisance to the world.

DOROTHY L. SAYERS

✦

Value work. But not any kind of work. Ask yourself, 'Is the work vital, strengthening my own character, or inspiring others, or helping the world?'

ANNA ROBERTSON BROWN

WORK SMART AND STICK IT OUT

Women have to be a lot smarter and brighter and
have to work a lot harder to prepare themselves.
They have to watch what they do and how they
behave. It's not a free world yet.

LETITIA BALDRIDGE

The test for whether or not you can hold
a job should not be the arrangement of
your chromosomes.

CONGRESSWOMAN BELLA ABZUG

Nighttime is really the best time to work. All the
ideas are there to be yours because everyone else
is asleep.

CATHERINE O'HARA

Hard work need not always be a chore.
At least not outside the house.

JENNIFER CROWLEY

All work done mindfully rounds us out, helps
complete us as persons.

MARSHA SINETAR

✦

When her last child is off to school, we don't want
the talented woman wasting her time in work
far below her capacity. We want her to come
out running.

MARY INGRAHAM BUNTING

✦

I am independent! I can live alone,
and I love to work.

MARY CASSATT

✦

I hate housework. You make the beds, you wash
the dishes, and six months later you have to start all
over again.

JOAN RIVERS

People have to feel needed. Frequently, we just
offer a job and 'perks.' We don't always offer
people a purpose. When people feel there is a
purpose and that they're needed, there's not much
else to do except let them do the work.

MAYA ANGELOU

The days you work are the best days.

GEORGIA O'KEEFFE

To work in the world lovingly means that we are
defining what we will be for, rather than reacting to
what we are against.

CHRISTINA BALDWIN

Personally, I have nothing against work, particularly
when performed quietly and unobtrusively by
someone else. I just don't happen to think it's an
appropriate subject for an "ethic."

BARBARA EHRENREICH

If hard work were such a wonderful thing, surely the rich would have kept it all to themselves.

LANE KIRKLAND

✦

Always be smarter than the people who hire you.

LENA HORNE

✦

Work is something you can count on, a trusted lifelong friend who never deserts you.

MARGARET BOURKE-WHITE

✦

Rather than sit around, I'll work.

KELLY LYNCH

✦

I work as often as I want and yet I'm free as a bird.

ETHEL MERMAN

...look and listen hard, do not be discouraged by rejections—we've all had them many times—and revise your work.

JOYCE CAROL OATES

Attempt the impossible in order to improve your work.

BETTE DAVIS

Aerodynamically the bumblebee shouldn't be able to fly, but the bumblebee doesn't know that, so it goes on flying anyway.

MARY KAY ASH

Yesterday I dared to struggle. Today I dare to win.

BERNADETTE DEVLIN

Plan your work for today and every day, then work your plan.

MARGARET THATCHER

There are two kinds of people, those who do the work and those who take credit. Try to be in the first group, there is less competition there.

INDIRA GANDHI

✦

Opportunities are often disguised as hard work, so most people don't recognize them.

ANN LANDERS

✦

I would rather make mistakes in kindness and compassion than work miracles in unkindness and hardness.

MOTHER TERESA

✦

Goals are dreams within deadlines.

DIANA SCHARF HUNT

Apply Some Elbow Grease

The biggest sin is sitting on your ass.

FLORYNCE KENNEDY

When it comes to getting things done, we need
fewer architects and more bricklayers.

COLLEEN C. BARRETT

By and large, mothers and housewives are the only
workers who do not have regular time off. They are
the great vacationless class.

ANNE MORROW LINDBERGH

✦

Don't feel entitled to anything you didn't
sweat and struggle for.

MARIAN WRIGHT EDELMAN

Nobody ever drowned in his own sweat.

ANN LANDERS

Luck? I don't know anything about luck. I've never banked on it, and I'm afraid of people who do. Luck to me is something else: hard work—and realizing what is opportunity and what isn't.

LUCILLE BALL

The only thing that ever sat its way to success was a hen.

SARAH BROWN

The sweat of hard work is not to be displayed. It is much more graceful to appear favored by the gods.

MAXINE HONG KINGSTON

✦

Whatever muscles I have are the product of my own hard work and nothing else.

EVELYN ASHFORD

Inspiration usually comes during work,
rather than before it.

MADELEINE L'ENGLE

Creativity comes from trust. Trust your instincts. And
never hope more than you work.

RITA MAE BROWN

I didn't have to work until I was three.
But after that, I never stopped.

MARTHA RAYE

About the only thing that comes to us
without effort is old age.

GLORIA PITZER

✦

Nothing will work unless you do.

MAYA ANGELOU

For the Love of It

Work is either fun or drudgery. It depends on your attitude. I like fun.

COLLEEN C. BARRETT

Career is too pompous a word. It was a job, and I have always felt privileged to be paid for what I love doing.

BARBARA STANWYCK

You know you are on the road to success if you would do your job and not be paid for it.

OPRAH WINFREY

All the things I love is what my business is about.

MARTHA STEWART

To love what you do and feel that it matters—how could anything be more fun?

KATHERINE GRAHAM

Your Goals Will Grow You

Make a list of short-term goals you would like to achieve by the end of the year, month, or even week. As you accomplish your goals, give gratitude for the effort, inspiration, people, and other factors that helped you along the way. My goal is to see how I can give more to those around me, near and far. I would love to hear your aspirations!

Chapter Nine

Never Hold Back: Shine Your Light Each and Every Day!

We all need reminders every now and then. You don't leap out of bed every day knowing you are amazing and about to have an incredible day. All of us have a lot of demands, pressures, to-do tasks, and responsibilities, so we find ourselves rushing around, working hard to please others. Most of the time, you find yourself at the back of your own bus, having made everyone else happy but your own damn self. Then you go and beat yourself up about it.

Let's stop that, shall we?

I'm here to remind you that you are pretty darn great. I had to learn to remind myself of that, but you know what? It feels pretty darn good. It is even kind of addictive in the best possible way. While this might seem like a fluffy little exercise, it actually runs quite deep and will serve you the rest of your life. There are reasons we need esteem boosters here and there; we pick up scars along the way and get bumps and bruises in the wake of the stress of daily life. If you had a bad childhood, you have these old "tapes" from poor parenting that loop around in your brain on an unconscious level: "You'll never amount to anything. You're not good at sports. Your sister has a much better singing voice than you, so we're sending her to music camp, and you can stay behind and babysit." Even really nice moms and dads perpetrate these parenting errors that leave marks on the souls of their children. So you need to make it one of your daily habits to keep affirming yourself. No matter what, keep forging ahead, knowing you are fabulous!

❧

Keep making great strides in the face of adversity. Holding down the fort while dreaming up the next great thing. Hurtling over massive barriers to your success with creative leaps and bounds. Just think: women have been doing this since the beginning of time, and it doesn't look to be slowing down any time soon. You may cram more into your day and get paid less for it, get fewer big breaks, and struggle to make your ideas heard, but you know what? You're up for this challenge.

But wait. In creeps fear, in slithers self-doubt. Are we more susceptible to these, too? Maybe so, because we're in tune with our feelings and those of the people around us. But we have to remember that the flip side of our self-doubt is our ability to empathize—the emotional intelligence that serves us in every relationship we have, from the bedroom to the boardroom. And let's be honest with ourselves. As Marianne Williamson put it so well, "Our deepest fear is not that we are inadequate. Our deepest fear is that we are powerful beyond measure." Know yourself, and don't hold back. Give yourself permission to find the best of you and let it shine without shame or apology. Nobody's going to benefit from your hesitation—you've got too much to get done to keep your talents hidden away so that others are more comfortable around you.

Dare to be powerful. Try it out. All those clichés—roll with the punches, just do it, you'll never know until you try, you can do anything you set your mind to—well, they get stuck in our heads because they're true. So go for it!

Believe in Yourself

To believe in something not yet proved and to underwrite it with our lives: it is the only way we can leave the future open.

LILLIAN SMITH

Only with a steady heart can true excellence be reached.

MOIRA LANDON

I can honestly say that I was never affected by the question of the success of an undertaking. If I felt it was the right thing to do, I was for it regardless of the possible outcome.

GOLDA MEIR

Everyone has talent. What is rare is the courage to follow talent to the dark place where it leads.

ERICA JONG

It's not so much how busy you are, but why you are busy. The bee is praised; the mosquito is swatted.

MARIE O'CONNER

Do not follow where the path may lead. Go instead where there is no path and leave a trail.

MURIEL STRODE

One must fight for a life of action, not reaction.

RITA MAE BROWN

A sobering thought: what if, at this very moment, I
am living up to my full potential?

JANE WAGNER

Women share with men the need for personal
success, even the taste of power, and no longer
are we willing to satisfy those needs through the
achievements of surrogates, whether husbands,
children, or merely role models.

ELIZABETH DOLE

Please know that I am quite aware of the hazards.
Women must try to do things as men have tried.
When they fail, their failure must be but a challenge
to others.

AMELIA EARHART

Ϟ

The most alluring thing a woman can have
is confidence.

BEYONCÉ KNOWLES-CARTER

Inaction, contrary to its reputation as being a refuge, is neither safe nor comfortable.

MADELINE KUHN

✦

Getting ahead in a difficult profession requires avid faith in yourself. That is why some people with mediocre talent, but with great inner drive, go much further than people with vastly superior talent.

SOPHIA LOREN

✦

It is above all by the imagination that we achieve perception and compassion and hope.

URSULA K. LE GUIN

✦

I have dreamed in my life, dreams that have stayed with me after, and changed my ideas; they have gone through and through me, like wine through water, and altered the color of my mind.

EMILY BRONTË

Believe in yourself: across all ages, studies have shown that a solid belief in one's own abilities increases life satisfaction by over 40 [percent] and makes us happier both in our work and home lives.

MEG DESMOND

Overcoming Challenges and Fears

You gain strength, courage, and confidence by every experience in which you really stop to look fear in the face…. You must do the thing you think you cannot do.

ELEANOR ROOSEVELT

You may be disappointed if you fail, but you are doomed if you don't try.

BEVERLY SILLS

✦

You can do one of two things: just shut up, which is something I don't find easy, or learn an awful lot very fast, which is what I tried to do.

JANE FONDA

If we are to achieve a richer culture, rich in contrasting values, we must recognize the whole gamut of human potentialities, and so weave a less arbitrary social fabric, one in which each diverse gift will find a fitting place.

MARGARET MEAD

It irritates me to be told how things have always been done. I defy the tyranny of precedent. I cannot afford the luxury of a closed mind. I go for anything that might improve the past.

CLARA BARTON

You can't build a reputation on what you intend to do.

LIZ SMITH

Success will come to you in direct proportion to the number of times you are willing to risk failure.

PAT GURITZ

Because I am a woman, I must make unusual efforts to succeed. If I fail, no one will say, 'She doesn't have what it takes.' They will say, 'Women don't have what it takes.'

CLARE BOOTHE LUCE

I really don't think life is about the I-could-have-beens. Life is only about the I-tried-to-do. I don't mind the failure, but I can't imagine that I'd forgive myself if I didn't try.

NIKKI GIOVANNI

A champion is afraid of losing. Everyone else is afraid of winning.

BILLIE JEAN KING

You'll never do a whole lot unless you're brave enough to try.

DOLLY PARTON

Risk! Risk anything! Care no more for the opinion of others, for those voices. Do the hardest thing on earth for you. Act for yourself. Face the truth.

KATHERINE MANSFIELD

When I dare to be powerful—to use my strength in the service of my vision—then it becomes less and less important whether or not I am afraid.

AUDRE LORDE

If you just set out to be liked, you would be prepared to compromise on anything at any time, and you would achieve nothing.

MARGARET THATCHER

Sweet Successes

Fearless women go to the top.

BEYONCÉ KNOWLES-CARTER

For what is done or learned by one class of women
becomes, by virtue of their common womanhood,
the property of all women.

ELIZABETH BLACKWELL

Not only have women been successful in entering
fields in which men are supposed to have a more
natural aptitude, but they have created entirely
new businesses.

LUCRETIA P. HUNTER

Winning may not be everything, but losing has little
to recommend it.

SENATOR DIANNE FEINSTEIN

The worst part of success is to try to find someone
who is happy for you.

BETTE MIDLER

The women of today are the thoughts of their mothers and grandmothers, embodied and made alive. They are active, capable, determined, and bound to win…millions of women dead and gone are speaking through us today.

MATILDA JOSLYN GAGE

Security is not the meaning of my life. Great opportunities are worth the risk.

SHIRLEY HUFSTEDLER

I don't think any change in the world has been more significant than the change in the status of women…. A woman's world was her home, her family, and perhaps a little community service. Today, a woman's world is as broad as the universe.

BELLE S. SPAFFORD

If I had learned to type, I never would have made brigadier general.

ELIZABETH P. HOISINGTOM

Don't confuse "things" with success—you are
neither better nor worse for where you live,
what you drive, or the size of your bank account.
Remember what really matters in your life—and it is
not "stuff."

MARY JANE RYAN

Getting to the top isn't bad, and it's probably best
done as an afterthought.

ANNE WILSON SCHAEF

Take Little Steps. Make Huge Strides

Success is not a doorway, it's a staircase.

DOTTIE WALTERS

I am only one; but still I am one. I cannot do
everything, but still I can do something. I will not
refuse to do the something I can do.

HELEN KELLER

We must not, in trying to think about how we can make a big difference, ignore the small daily differences we can make, which over time add up to big differences that we often cannot foresee.

MARIAN WRIGHT EDELMAN

Don't wait for your ship to come in and feel angry and cheated when it doesn't. Get going with something small.

IRENE KASSORLA

How wonderful it is that nobody needs to wait a single moment before starting to improve the world.

ANNE FRANK

Do not wait for leaders; do it alone, person to person.

MOTHER TERESA

I'm always moving forward.

DEBBIE ALLEN

I believe the choice to be excellent begins with aligning your thoughts and words with the intention to require more from yourself.

OPRAH WINFREY

Strive for excellence, each and every day.

MARION CONDIT

Never Give Up

Just don't give up trying to do what you really want to do. Where there is love and inspiration, I don't think you can go wrong.

ELLA FITZGERALD

Always continue the climb. It is possible for you to do whatever you choose, if you first get to know who you are and are willing to work with a power that is greater than ourselves to achieve it.

ELLA WHEELER WILCOX

Something which we think is impossible now is not impossible in another decade.

CONSTANCE BAKER MOTLEY

When I stand before God at the end of my life, I would hope that I would not have a single bit of talent left and could say, "I used everything you gave me."

ERMA BOMBECK

I never see what has been done; I only see what remains to be done.

MARIE CURIE

The way I see it, if you want the rainbow, you gotta put up with the rain.

DOLLY PARTON

✦

Human successes, like human failures, are composed of one action at a time and achieved by one person at a time.

PATSY H. SAMPSON

I think one's feelings waste themselves in words;
they ought all to be distilled into actions which
bring results.

FLORENCE NIGHTINGALE

The only sin is mediocrity.

MARTHA GRAHAM

Perseverance is failing nineteen times and
succeeding the twentieth.

JULIE ANDREWS

Learning is not attained by chance, it must be
sought for with ardor and diligence.

ABIGAIL ADAMS

I'm not going to limit myself because people won't
accept the fact that I can do something else.

DOLLY PARTON

No matter how tough, no matter what kind of outside pressure, no matter how many bad breaks along the way, I must keep my sights on the final goal, to win…with more love and passion than the world has ever witnessed in any performance.

BILLIE JEAN KING

If you don't like something, change it. If you can't change it, change your attitude. Don't complain.

MAYA ANGELOU

There's a big difference between seeing an opportunity and seizing an opportunity.

PAT GURITZ

We can do anything we want to do if we stick with it long enough.

HELEN KELLER

Do You Know How Great You Are

Compliment someone today, and mean it. A genuine compliment can boost someone's confidence and that is a great feeling. If you like your coworker's blouse or new haircut (or both!), tell her. Open and honest communication works wonders for developing relationships and makes everybody's day a little bit nicer. Take the time to let someone know that you appreciate having her or him in your life. Sometimes we forget how good it feels to be appreciated, yet we know how lousy it feels to be unappreciated. Go ahead and tell someone how thankful you are for her or his presence in your life; it will only make you closer. Wonderful things can happen when you affirm the people in your life.

CONCLUSION

Three Life-Changing Pieces of Advice
I Am Passing on to You

In closing, I want to give you the three best pieces of advice
I have ever received. One is to get up earlier each day, the
second is to stop complaining, and the last is about being
grateful, no matter what.

Get Up a Half Hour Earlier Each Day

This simple suggestion from Peter Shankman at a publishing
conference ended up being a life-changing piece of advice.
He said when he tried this, it transformed his life, and it is as
simple as this: get up a half hour earlier, and use that time to
reach out to people. He said it can be as easy as wishing a
happy birthday to your Facebook contacts, one meaningful
phone call first thing in the morning, or writing a personal
note to someone you have longed to be in contact with. I
remember listening to him and thinking that I really didn't
want to get up any earlier, that my days were long enough,
and that it did not sound that appealing. But his sincerity
and enthusiasm somehow broke through my "baditude,"
and I pondered the idea as I walked back to my car and

drove across the Bay Bridge back to my office. I decided to try it, and I can tell you, he is *right*.

That extra half hour every morning has been one of the best investments I've ever made, so much so that I added an hour. It completely changed my life for the better. Try it!

STOP COMPLAINING

Go one day without complaining; even better, go a week. If this is hard for you to accomplish, it's time to make some changes in your life. Think positively, live in the present, and appreciate where you are and who you are. Today is a gift. Accept and embrace it. Mark Bowen authored a fantastic book on this very topic, which I turn to when I need a reminder, as all of us do now and again. My copy came with a bracelet—a simple way to monitor how often you complain that helps you track your progress toward becoming "complaint-free." Put on the bracelet, and every time you complain, switch it to the other wrist. The goal is to go twenty-one consecutive days without complaining or switching the side where you wear the bracelet. It is harder than you might think, and I was a bit shocked at what a complainer I turned out to be. It was a really good exercise for me, and I highly recommend it. I benefited enormously from it, and I suspect the people around me did too!

Have an Attitude of Gratitude

1. Be grateful and recognize the things others have done to help you.

2. When you say "Thank you" to someone, it signals what you appreciate and why you appreciate it.

3. Post a "Thank you to all" on your Facebook page or your blog, or send individual emails to friends, family, and colleagues.

4. Send a handwritten thank-you note. These are noteworthy because so few of us take time to write and mail them in our modern age.

5. Think thoughts of gratitude—two or three good things that happened today—and notice how calm settles through your head, at least for a moment. It activates a part of the brain that floods the body with endorphins, or feel-good hormones.

6. Remember the ways your life has been made easier or better because of others' efforts. Be aware of and acknowledge the good things, large and small, going on around you.

7. Keep a gratitude journal, or set aside time each day or evening to list the people or things you're grateful for today. The list may start out short, but it will grow as you notice more of the good things around you.

8. Being grateful shakes you out of self-absorption and helps you recognize those who've done wonderful things for you. Expressing that gratitude continues to draw those people into your sphere.

9. Remember this thought from Maya Angelou: "When you learn, teach; when you get, give."

10. Join forces to do good. If you have survived illness or loss, you may want to reach out to others to help as a way of showing gratitude for those who reached out to you.

About the Author

Becca Anderson comes from a long line of preachers and teachers from Ohio and Kentucky. The teacher side of her family led Becca to become a women's studies scholar who writes *The Blog of Awesome Women*. An avid collector of meditations, prayers, and blessings, she helps run a "Gratitude and Grace Circle" that meets monthly at homes, churches, and bookstores. Becca Anderson credits her spiritual practice with helping in her recovery from cancer and wants to share this with anyone who is facing difficulty in their life. The author of *Think Happy to Stay Happy*, *Real Life Mindfulness*, and *Every Day Thankful*, Becca Anderson shares her inspirational writings and suggested acts of kindness at https://thedailyinspoblog.wordpress.com.

Mango Publishing, established in 2014, publishes an eclectic list of books by diverse authors — both new and established voices — on topics ranging from business, personal growth, women's empowerment, LGBTQ studies, health, and spirituality to history, popular culture, time management, decluttering, lifestyle, mental wellness, aging, and sustainable living. We were recently named 2019's #1 fastest growing independent publisher by *Publishers Weekly*. Our success is driven by our main goal, which is to publish high quality books that will entertain readers as well as make a positive difference in their lives.

Our readers are our most important resource; we value your input, suggestions, and ideas. We'd love to hear from you — after all, we are publishing books for you!

Please stay in touch with us and follow us at:

Facebook: Mango Publishing
Twitter: @MangoPublishing
Instagram: @MangoPublishing
LinkedIn: Mango Publishing
Pinterest: Mango Publishing

Sign up for our newsletter at www.mango.bz and receive a free book!

Join us on Mango's journey to reinvent publishing, one book at a time.